GLORY OVER CALVARY

GLORY OVER CALVARY

Peter Trumper

Evangelical Press of Wales

© Evangelical Press of Wales, 1994
First published 1994
ISBN 1 85049 112 7

Cover design: Rhiain M. Davies

Published by the Evangelical Press of Wales
Bryntirion, Bridgend, Mid Glamorgan CF31 4DX
Printed in Wales by D. Brown & Sons Ltd., Bridgend

CONTENTS

FOREWORD

*'The cross is the centre of the world's history. The
incarnation of Christ and the crucifixion
of our Lord are the pivot round which all
the events of the ages revolve.'*
Alexander Maclaren

A companion volume to *They Beheld His Glory* (1990), this is
preaching in print—preaching on the big themes of the cross and
incarnation, the 'old, old story' retold in a fresh and challenging
way. The author looks at the cross through the eyes of those who
were there, imaginatively but not speculatively. Each character
study is well researched and provides the reader with a wealth of
background information. Above all, Christ is exalted in his person
and work as the only Saviour of sinners.

Twenty-five years ago as a schoolboy in Pembrokeshire God
met with me savingly through one of Peter Trumper's sermons. In
commending this book to you, my prayer is that you too will meet
the Saviour here.

DAVID JONES

PREFACE

At 9.00 a.m. on a Friday, about the year AD 29, the sounds of hammering could be heard just beyond the city walls of Jerusalem. The most significant event in the history of the world was due to take place. It was the day that they crucified Jesus of Nazareth.

We can only guess what passed through his mind those first few moments on the bloodied cross, thoughts which vied for attention with the pain he was enduring. Certainly, they would have been directed towards heaven as he sought comfort from his Father's love. He had experienced it unreservedly, unceasingly, throughout eternal ages past where he had been 'daily his delight, rejoicing always before him'. Divine love permeates the eternal mysteries: the unhindered outpouring of pure affection between the three persons of the Godhead. It is 'vast, unmeasured, boundless, free'.

By contrast, Jesus looked out upon the malevolence in front of him: the wicked priests, the hardened soldiers, the mocking bystanders. Even his two fellow victims on either side of him did not refrain from abuse. Every aching limb and muscular spasm added their weight to the blasphemous mockery and unbelieving jibes aimed at him as satanic darts.

As the moments passed, Jesus slowly became aware of a profound sensation of excruciating despair and torment, far outweighing his physical sufferings, which welled up from deep within him. Blackness of the deepest hue descended upon his soul, as sin in all its loathsomeness enveloped it. Sins, merely 'covered' from centuries of legal offerings, ascended from the depths of ancient times directed to their destination by the Father himself.

Together with these were sins which had already been committed in thought, word and deed by Jesus' contemporaries, and those which were yet to be conceived until the end of time. They flew to the cross and found a similar resting place. A fearful spirit of ultimate desolation gripped his soul, causing him to shout aloud, 'My God, my God, why hast thou forsaken me?' (Matthew 27:46).

Jesus' soul had been hurled into the vortex of eternal wrath.

The sacrificial Lamb of God was ripped open and 'flayed' by the almighty hands of the Father, his 'knife' slicing and cutting to the bone, reaching for the least particle of sin tissue. The fierce light of burning holiness searched every niche of Christ's soul, and the Father wreaked vengeance at will without respite or mercy against everything he found there. When the task had been completed to his satisfaction, then could it be said that the power of sin had been broken. Only at that point did heaven acknowledge that sin's stain had been erased, and the sinner set free.

In short, the Lamb was experiencing the torments of eternal retribution which the elect deserve. The 'terrors of law and of God' were felt that day by the Son, the appointed substitute for sinners who had dared to break the moral law without restraint. Almighty God, resplendent in perfect righteousness, had been offended. By Christ's passive obedience on the cross, both God and his commandments were satisfied. At the same time, Satan and sin were dealt a blow from which there could be no recovery, and satanic principalities were triumphantly overthrown.

For hours, the 'altar flames' leaped high around the soul of Christ, the burning 'heat' of eternal indignation having reached its fullest intensity. The Lamb of God experienced what was unique to himself. As the final and smallest fragments of the sacrificial offerings always slithered through the grating of the altar of burnt offering, the figure hanging on the cross had reached his lowest ebb. Christ had given everything, his whole being sapped of all strength, for he could not give more than his life. His blood had been poured out into the fountain 'for sin and for uncleanness'. With seconds left, Jesus gasped triumphantly, 'IT IS FINISHED' (John 19:30).

At that moment heaven was filled with a paean of praise, every recess resounding to everlasting songs of exultation. It was the eternal 'day of gladness' when 'silver trumpets' blew in grateful recognition that Christ's work was completed, and that God had made his peace with sinners. Good will indeed (Luke 2:14)! It was the day when glory shone over Calvary.

1

THE INQUISITIVE SPECTATOR

'And they compelled one Simon a Cyrenian, who passed
by, coming out of the country, the father of Alexander
and Rufus, to bear his cross'
(Mark 15:21).

The Jews swarmed to the major feasts in Jerusalem like bees to a honey pot. Weary travellers bustled in throngs at the city gates. Donkeys, mules, heavily laden camels, exhausted children, impatient parents, heat, flies, dust and grime: the discomfort was evident. As many as two and a half million people descended upon Jerusalem three times annually for the festivities. They arrived from every area of Israel, and from throughout the known world, as on the most memorable feast of Pentecost (Acts 2:5-11). Only the presence of Roman militia stood between the pilgrims and chaos. Yet, despite the difficulties, the feasts were anticipated with great excitement.

Amidst the jostling crowds on the first Good Friday was a man called Simon. He, his wife and children were members of the very large Jewish community in Cyrene (Tripoli, Libya), a colony at one time so strong it had rebelled against the Romans during the Maccabean wars. As a consequence, the Cyrenian Jews gained an influence far beyond their homeland.

The journey from Cyrene to Jerusalem would have taken a long time, for there was no comfortable mode of transport. Only slow progress could be made over rough and uncertain terrain. The weariness of the journey, however, was offset by conversations among the adults, the women riding the spare donkeys and the men leading the pack mules, while the youngsters amused themselves as they ran and danced alongside.

The travellers sang psalms in anticipation of the festive rejoicing to be experienced in Jerusalem, where old friends of the synagogue waited to greet them as they did three times a year. On this occasion, though, Simon and his family little realized what lay ahead for them. Their entire lives were soon to be completely changed.

At each Passover feast in Jerusalem, the Temple area was vibrant with activity, and the sounds and smells of stock awaiting slaughter in their pens and cages. Bullocks, lambs, goats, doves and pigeons were sacrificed in accordance to the law and the worshipper's means. Most chose to offer a lamb. In fact, as many as 260,000 paschal lambs were sacrificially slain in the Temple precincts during the Passover feast. This massive undertaking traditionally took place on the day of the first spring full moon. That is, on the fourteenth day of the month Abib (Nisan).

The entire operation had to be efficiently handled by the authorities to cope with the crush. The queues were long, consisting of several divisions of a thousand men apiece who were allowed entry into the courtyard. As each batch of a thousand offerings was slaughtered, trumpets blew heralding the fact, and another division entered. Each man paid his annual sacred tribute of half a shekel. No foreign currency was accepted, which gave the money-changers much to do in coping with the migrant worshippers.

His task having been completed, Simon left the Temple with the intention of returning to his family. During the festival they were staying outside Jerusalem in the country because the city was so crowded. Later that day he would have had to return to the court of the priests to collect the carcass, for once slain the lambs were hung on hooks to allow the blood to drain away. The sacrifice was then flayed and the fat separated, before being offered with incense upon the altar. Only then would Simon have been able to take the meat to his wife for cleaning and cooking, in readiness for the Passover meal that evening. However, his plans were delayed for some time.

He was distracted by the roar of excited crowds coming from the direction of Antonia fortress, the governor's residence during the festivities. With many others, he was drawn towards the noise.

Once there he was confronted with a gruesome spectacle. Three men were lurching towards him, each bowed under the weight of heavy crossbeams lying along their shoulders, and to which their arms were tied. A centurion stood close by, cane in hand. Everyone knew where they were heading. It was Golgotha, the place of the skull (Matthew 27:33). The three men were due to be executed.

Simon had witnessed scenes like this before on many occasions, both in Jerusalem as well as in Cyrene. They were an ugly, but regular, feature of everyday life under Roman rule. Executions were commonplace, especially in Jerusalem during the feast days. Yet, this time, he felt there was a difference because of the attention the three victims had attracted. The area was unusually crowded, with inquisitive onlookers jostling with each other for a better view. Simon found himself equally attentive. It is a sad aspect of fallen man's nature that he is tempted to gape at the sufferings of others.

As the wretched party drew alongside, he noticed the ravages scourging had made upon the men hunched under the crossbeams. Their backs formed a network of deep ruts, oozing blood. The centurion did not appear to notice, but continually applied his cane to the same sensitive areas. Other soldiers in the group increased the assault with lashes, curses and kicks as it made its slow and painful way towards the place of execution just beyond the city walls. All this time, the jostling mob kept up a continuous barrage of frenzied shouts, unable to contain itself. The blood-letting and savagery had kindled within it a fearful and crazed spirit.

The centurion was having problems keeping the procession moving. One of the exhausted men kept falling to his knees, the heavy crossbeam making it difficult for him to remain upright. The cobbled ground was no cushion for his face, and Simon could see the effect. Blood trickled from the man's nose, and fresh splinters from the beam entered an already badly chafed neck.

Each time this happened, as the soldiers roughly and impatiently jerked the man to his feet, his companions in this drama were equally angry with him. The wooden beams were getting heavier as their bodies grew weaker, and the constant delays made matters worse. The man staggered on for a brief moment before sinking to his knees again. Eventually, his body unable to resist any more blows, he collapsed and remained on the ground breathing heavily.

Simon had noticed something else. Criminals within the shadow of execution, knowing they had nothing to lose, always sought to go down fighting and cursing. If their helpless situation prevented retaliation, their parched tongues gave vent to their feelings. The air was thick with oaths and vile language. However, the stranger causing the slow passage of the procession made no effort to retaliate (1 Peter 2:23).

Both mystified and impressed, Simon asked his neighbour who the stranger was. It would have been the natural thing for him to do. On his visits to Jerusalem, Simon had often heard rumours about a certain man claiming to be the Messiah. So this was the Carpenter from Nazareth!

It was clear that Jesus could go no further unassisted, the hours of suffering having taken their toll. A strong man was required to carry the timber. The centurion glanced around at the crowds. He saw Simon who, guessing what the centurion intended, attempted to push his way through those milling around him. He had not gone far when he was seized by the soldiers and obliged to obey the officer's command. Simon made his protest but to no avail, the Romans being expert at compelling people to submit.

Suddenly, the burly Cyrenian found himself involved in a drama which at the time he would not have understood. Having slain the paschal lamb for his family, with the blood stains probably still visible on him, he was unknowingly drawn by Providence to the side of the bleeding Paschal Lamb! This unique experience was to bring salvation to Simon and his family, and one partially mirrored in the apostle Paul's prayer: 'That I may know him . . . and the fellowship of his sufferings, being made conformable unto his death' (Philippians 3:10). Simon had stepped from the sidelines as a mere inquisitive spectator into the cauldron with Christ. He was about to learn what it meant to be a Christian.

To begin with, he had been especially selected to follow the Son of God. Even though he had resisted the command, nevertheless he discovered he was obliged to heed it. Like blind Bartimaeus (Mark 10:46-52), or the diminutive Zacchaeus (Luke 19:1-10), Simon was also providentially compelled to follow the Saviour. The crossbeam was embraced. It was similar to the Christian's experience who, compelled by grace, identifies himself with his Lord's suffering and does so gladly for the rest of his life (Galatians 2:20).

Had they stopped to think about it, many of those caught up in the events would have remembered Jesus' startling words on this subject not long before. As he was making his way to Jerusalem for the final time (Luke 9:51) vast crowds followed him, but Jesus was not impressed. He knew the fickle hearts of men (John 2:24,25). Quantity never excited Jesus. Quality did. As the people crowded him on that occasion, he addressed them sternly: 'whosoever doth not bear his cross, and come after me, cannot be my disciple' (Luke 14:27). The final chilling words 'cannot be my disciple' were repeated twice more.

In the meantime, Simon found himself illustrating the dilemma of discipleship. With his wife and children waiting for him to return, and wondering what had become of him, he served Jesus at their expense. For those rare moments he understood what it meant to place Jesus first; to 'hate' his family. Likewise, confronted by the crowd's antagonism and the indifferent brutality of the soldiers, he was forced to 'hate . . . his own life also'. There was no possibility of escape. Simon forsook 'all', walking in Jesus' footsteps *en route* to Calvary. He did not appreciate the irony at the time, but his action hastened the Saviour's arrival at his destination where he was due to bear Simon's far heavier burden of sin!

He had only been an innocent bystander drawn into the affray, yet he was not spared a further lesson in discipleship. It was the hardest one of all. He had to remain in Jesus' shadow at whatever the cost to his pride, sharing in the general humiliation and indignities suffered by the Lord. Simon was not excused merely because he had been a spectator. The occasion was no respecter of persons, or of sensitivities.

The sun by this time was rising steadily. Exhaustion was having its effect. The discomfort was heightened by the atmosphere which surrounded him. The way to the city gate, beyond which lay the hill Calvary, was along an avenue of angry faces and gesticulating arms. The hands which had clasped palm leaves a few days earlier, as Jesus had ridden triumphantly into Jerusalem, were now clenched fists beating the air.

They had offered their sacrifices in the Temple precincts, and in the evening would be seated around the table with their families eating the Passover meal. Yet on that Good Friday morning these same Jews were engaged in the humiliation and death of God's Son. Most of them had earlier shouted to Pilate, 'his blood be on us, and on our children' (Matthew 27:25). Such is the fickleness of human nature, and the depth of its depravity.

Simon had watched similar and equally degrading spectacles before, but he never imagined he would be in the centre of one. The atmosphere was particularly horrendous. Satan had tried to kill Jesus at his birth (Matthew 2:16), as well as earlier in his ministry (Luke 4:29). Now he revealed his undoubted presence in the Sanhedrin's guile, Rome's cruelty and in the viciousness of ordinary people. The crack of the whips, the curses of the soldiers and the baying of the pitiless crowds were fearsome reminders of what it meant to be confronted by satanically controlled hatred.

The atmosphere was reminiscent of the psalmist's words relating to the Messiah's agony: 'The sorrows of death compassed me, and the floods of ungodly men made me afraid. The sorrows of hell compassed me about: the snares of death went before me' (Psalm 18:4,5). In the light of this, one can easily imagine Simon's feelings in his unusual and unique experience. Hell swirled around him, and acute loneliness swept over him. It must have appeared to him that he was taking part in a nightmare. He missed his wife and children and worried about them, as they by this time must have wondered what had become of him. At least he comforted himself with the fact that Golgotha would soon be reached and, unlike his companions, he would be permitted to return home.

How long the journey seemed! It could only have been a short time since they had started out along this route, but with the continual delays and uninterrupted strain it appeared like hours. By now, Simon had had time to assess his companions. The two criminals were replying to the situation as only they knew how, shouting verbal abuse in all directions as they lurched from side to side. They also fell occasionally upon the cobbled ground, and were brutally jerked to their feet again under the 'encouragements' of renewed lashings.

Those who share suffering invariably discover the common bond of friendship, but Simon would have noticed that was not so on this occasion. Jesus was isolated from the other two men. They shared a common background and outlook on life. The silent Jesus, 'a man of sorrows and acquainted with grief' (Isaiah 53:3), was by comparison a solitary figure. His quiet demeanour, even under extreme pressure, was the key which unlocked the mystery behind Simon's bewilderment.

He would have been undoubtedly intrigued by Jesus' behaviour, and it led to his eventual salvation. Throughout the ordeal Jesus refrained from expressing his feelings, except for one brief moment when Simon heard him speaking to a group of professional mourners. The solemn words were so impressive that Simon committed them to memory (Luke 23:28-31). It was his final sermon, foretelling the downfall of Jerusalem in AD 70, the day of the 'dry tree'. The Son of God having been finally rejected by Israel, retribution from heaven would fall upon the city. A Roman invasion! – the sounds of battering rams and the ominous shrill of deadly missiles would one day be heard (Luke 19:43,44).

The pronouncement was delivered under intense physical and emotional strain through dry cracked lips, and a tongue swollen with dehydration. For a message to have been delivered in those circumstances, it must have been a vital one. The warnings of a dying man are always worth noting, especially from One whose presence and actions had stirred the conscience of Israel. Only a few heard the brief appeal, the clamour being so acute, but Simon was one of them. It made a profound impression upon him.

At last the procession arrived at its destination. Simon and his companions collapsed on the grassy knoll as the beams were cut from their numbed arms. As he waited, he had an opportunity to glance around. The forbidding place was correctly named, that of a skull, associated more with the dead than the living. It was the official place of execution, which engendered fear in the minds of Jerusalem's citizens. Those who were led the fatal half mile or so from the Praetorium to that spot outside the city wall never returned. People spoke guardedly about the horrors experienced there: of the anguished cries as men hung on crosses under the sky in torment and despair for hours, or even days, and in all weather conditions.

The centurion ordered his men to assemble the three crosses. With an increasing sense of horror Simon watched the Roman soldiers go about their tasks with the efficiency of those who had carried them out many times before. Soon, the sounds of hammering disturbed the gloomy atmosphere with a chilling reminder of the agony which was to follow.

The crosses having been prepared to receive their occupants, with the wooden beams securely fixed to the uprights, Simon saw Jesus and his equally exhausted companions harshly ordered to submit still further to the process of crucifixion. Arms and legs were bound with thick twine which pinioned them tightly to the crosses, chafing their already bleeding backs resting heavily upon the splintered wood. With every move they made, and with each passing hour, the twine would cut deeper into their weakened flesh. There was for Jesus, however, an even deeper agony to be endured. From childhood he had known the words of the messianic psalm, 'they pierced my hands and my feet' (Psalm 22:16).

The penetration of a heavy metal nail into thick flesh would not have been a straightforward operation, nor one which could be accomplished quickly. Each hammer blow was struck with great force, producing the expected loud agonized groan. The dull thud was enough to turn the stomachs of all but the most hardened.

When, at last, one numbed hand had been secured to the crossbeam it was then the turn of the other. The merciless task completed, there were still two feet to receive the same treatment.

After what must have seemed an interminable period to Simon, the crosses were ready for lifting into position. The soldiers dragged each one, with its victim firmly in place, until the base found the required slot in the ground. Then with a shuddering jolt the crosses stood upright, causing the twine to tighten and lacerate the bleeding flesh. Jesus' hands and feet pulled against the nails. Fresh blood flowed. The scene at Calvary echoed to the sounds of men in acute pain. Numbness quickly made way for unrelieved muscle cramp. Golgotha was no place for the faint-hearted.

Simon may have secretly breathed a sigh of relief that one of the crosses was not his. What must the victims have been thinking at that moment? Anyone in his position would have wished to help them, but there was no way in which he could. A dreadful finality hovered menacingly over the area.

He would not have been permitted to rest for long. He had fulfilled his task, and unauthorized spectators were not permitted to remain. However, one could not imagine Simon leaving the spot without a backward glance at the One whose cross he had carried. At the same time, it is unthinkable to believe that Jesus refused a smile in thanking him. As Simon returned to the city his thoughts were of the day's events thus far, and it was only shortly after nine o'clock in the morning!

It was a remarkable providence which brought Jesus and Simon together along the two entirely different paths chosen for them: the Son of God, the 'heir of all things', and the ordinary Jew from humble circumstances. Both had journeyed to Jerusalem for a purpose, the sinner to offer his family's paschal lamb and the Paschal Lamb Himself to be sacrificed for sinners. In the city their paths crossed, the Cyrenian and the Carpenter accompanying each other to Calvary within the most significant and solemn few hours in history.

As far as is known, no words were exchanged between them; yet a silent bond was formed. Nobody assisted Jesus without gaining a unique blessing from it. Even a Samaritan woman, one of the Jews' traditional enemies, received much more than she could have dreamed after Jesus had requested some water from her pitcher (John 4:1-30). As with Simon, the encounter rather than the deed led to her salvation.

There was much to tell his family when at last he returned to it, his sons Alexander and Rufus no doubt requesting the retelling of the account on numerous occasions! It was an astonishing story. Their father had actually accompanied the long-awaited Messiah during the fulfilment of his mission.

They had heard a great deal about Jesus during their visits to Jerusalem for the feasts over the previous three years, although they had refused to believe in him. As a family, they would have shared the general antagonism of the Cyrenian Jewish community towards Jesus and his disciples. Its members were numbered among those who opposed the godly Stephen, the first Christian martyr (Acts 6:9).

As the vast crowds later streamed from the city, there was much to think about. Usually the long journey home was spent as it had begun, in conversation and psalm singing, but on this occasion there was much more to consider and excite the curiosity of all the travellers.

Simon particularly had good reasons for reflection. His brief period spent with Jesus had changed his life, and later that of his family. So much so, they left the Jewish stronghold of Cyrene and lived in Rome, where they became well-known in Christian circles. In fact, when Mark's Gospel was written he mentioned both Simon and his children, assuming every Christian in the city would know them (Mark 15:21). Certainly the apostle Paul did, very affectionately (Romans 16:13).

The travellers had many other matters to think about. They had felt the impact of the earthquakes which had shaken Jerusalem and had shared the astonishment with everyone else when the land was strangely overcast with shadows. They had heard rumours of miraculous events: of the tearing of the Temple veil in the holy place, and of the dead rising in the cemeteries. Above all, of mysterious incidents taking place in the garden where Jesus' body had been buried, and of the empty tomb. The many questions were soon to be answered.

2

THE ASTONISHED CENTURION

'Certainly this was a righteous man'
(Luke 23:47).
'Truly this man was the Son of God'
(Mark 15:39).

A centurion, of which there were fifty-nine in a legion consisting
of 5,500 highly trained soldiers, was viewed by his men with a
mixture of emotions, but brotherly love would not have been one
of them. They might have respected his long slow climb up the
military ladder, admired his ability in hand-to-hand combat or his
charismatic leadership, but his reputation for stern if not brutal
discipline prevented any positive feelings towards him. The scars
which legionaries bore testified to the efficiency of the vine cane
in every centurion's hand, employed to beat them to death in the
extremity of desertion or rank disobedience.

In short, the centurion who has gone down in history as the
spectator of Christ's crucifixion was, as a leader of uncouth soldiers and experienced in the heat of battle, a hard man and unlikely
to be emotionally disturbed by what he saw. He was merely a non-
commissioned officer doing his job, who just 'happened' to be on
duty the day of history's greatest moment.

When the day had begun, as far as he and his men were concerned, it was going to be yet another crucifixion day. The
Romans had many of them. They were often detailed to conduct
the baser sort of men to the sombre place of execution. The regularity with which such occasions took place only served to dull
their sensitivities to them.

In the light of this, of all the witnesses to Jesus' atoning work
that historic day, the anonymous centurion was among the most
significant. Nobody could suggest he was other than an impartial

observer. As officer in charge of the proceedings, he was closer to Jesus than anyone else. He had supervised the assembling of the crosses and the crucifixion itself, and had watched as his three victims were raised into position. He saw the twisted expressions on their faces, heard their groans and cries, as their aching muscles bore the strain. Nothing would have escaped his notice.

In the light of that, and as a result of hours spent in his company, the centurion's audible comments were an astonishing and unbiased estimation demanding acknowledgement. This uncultured soldier was so convicted in his conscience and stirred in spirit that he believed he was looking at 'a righteous man', even 'the Son of God'.

The radical change in his thinking would not have come easily. He was a proud Roman, a significant cog in a well-oiled and efficient military machine owing its allegiance to no one except the most feared and powerful dictator in the known world. The Roman conquest of a land subjugated it to Caesar's rule and enslaved its inhabitants. It was therefore prudent, if one had the right social connections and could afford it, to gain the honour of being a citizen of Rome. How advantageous it was to be part of Imperium Romanum, as the apostle Paul discovered on more than one occasion! (See, for example, Acts 25:11,12.)

Roman pride, though, was not confined to the Eternal City standing securely in magnificent splendour on the banks of the Tiber. It spread itself to every corner of the empire. Nor was it solely a pride in its citizenship but in much more besides: administration, military might and commerce. The centurion, therefore, felt justified in feeling proud.

Arrogance always follows in pride's wake. He would have been contemptuous of those enslaved by Rome, the conquered territories like Israel. In any case, he was part of the occupying army merely carrying out orders. He certainly would not have volunteered for duty in such a barren land. There was nothing attractive about the place for one used to seeing the grandeur of Rome. We do not know where his home was, but he must have often longed to be back there, far removed from the dirt, dust, heat and sweat of foreign territory where he and his kind were the objects of intense loathing. For these reasons, he looked upon the sufferings of his three victims with complete indifference.

There is no reason why the centurion should have been different from any other Roman at the time, sharing in the prevailing spiritual emptiness. One thing is certain: his sudden exclamations upon seeing Jesus die were not superficial. They were made after a great deal of contemplation, made possible by the time spent in Jesus' company that horrendous day of crucifixion. He would not have understood, any more than the thieves, the theological significance of it all. But, with Simon of Cyrene, he knew he was in the presence of a most extraordinary person.

The first intimation that this was so was the moment Jesus was handed over to him. The prophet was correct when he said of the Messiah, 'there is no beauty that we should desire him' (Isaiah 53:2), but that would not have included the beauty of holiness. If, after being with God, Moses was obliged to cover his facial radiance with a veil, would not the grace of Christ have had an effect upon even the most bestial of Roman soldiers? It did upon those who arrived in the garden of Gethsemane to arrest him (John 18:6), an account which no doubt circulated in the barracks.

Then the procession moved off. The backcloth of ugly depravity which rippled through the menacing crowds, ruffian Romans and cursing thieves brought Jesus' bearing into sharp focus. The swish of the centurion's cane, the crack of whips, the insistent demands, the pushing and shoving: these were not sufficient to produce from Jesus any form of physical response. Yet it was not weakness the centurion noted, but meekness, the spirit of lowliness which is born of spiritual power.

He understood power in terms of the thump of the battering ram, the clash of daggers or the devastation caused by the catapult. He recognized it in the formation of the legions, marching beneath the standards bearing the insignia of the Roman eagle. Now he was observing another kind of power, unaffected by the efficiency of a war machine or the companionship of comrades, and one which drew upon hidden reserves deep within the soul.

The centurion was in the centre of the stage, and at the most passionate part of the drama. He must often have witnessed heroic courage from the most wicked of men on occasions like this, but the strength Jesus possessed did not arise from the grit and determination heroes summon up in trying circumstances. Commendable though those qualities are, meekness is of a finer and more profound kind. Jesus was capable of reacting contrary to normal human behaviour, which is to retaliate when oppressed.

The officer watched Jesus receive the blows, not without flinching, but submissively. This had been his entire approach throughout the long, weary hours when abused by the Jews and then by the Romans. Such was the impression created, the impact so indelibly marked upon the memory, that years later the apostle Peter commented upon it to Christians undergoing persecution. They were to remember their Lord's example, 'who, when he was reviled, reviled not again; when he suffered, he threatened not' (1 Peter 2:23).

Peter reminded his suffering brethren and sisters of the source of this impressive strength, these hidden resources: 'he threatened not, but committed himself to him that judgeth righteously' (1 Peter 2:23). The converted Saul, later the apostle Paul, yearned to enter even more deeply into this mystery, as does every committed Christian. If the apostle John 'beheld' the divine glory in Jesus, the pagan centurion was also deeply stirred by what he saw, even though at the time he could not define it.

But submission to his circumstances was only a part of what the Roman noticed about Jesus' behaviour. There was also a gracious aspect, a boundary over which only those indwelt by his Spirit can pass. Not only did he fail to retaliate – an act not limited to Christians – but he responded in a loving manner, even forgiving his tormentors. It was an example he had insisted his followers should emulate, and one which enables the Christian ethic to soar above the ordinary. In the death of the first Christian martyr, it was this gracious Christian principle which Stephen displayed (Acts 7:59,60).

The centurion would have noticed another facet. He had attended many crucifixions before, but never one like this. It was always unpleasant work, but the prisoners normally suffered and died unremembered. This occasion would have passed the same way, except for the fact that Jesus cast a massive silhouette over the entire proceedings. There was no place on the hill, nor in Israel itself, where one could forget that Jesus of Nazareth was being put to death.

Far from the situation overwhelming him, as it would have done had he been a charlatan, he appeared to control it with the display of the meekness he taught would one day 'inherit the earth' (Matthew 5:5). Paradoxically, Jesus was the eternal high priest allowing himself to be interrogated by the temporal high priest, the divine judge being judged, the conquering Word of God who 'was God' humbly tolerating personal abuse.

He was also the captive who 'imprisoned' Pilate in his own questions, the prey who tormented Herod the hunter with his tantalizing silence, and the abused victim who in the blackest moments of his dying agonies sought forgiveness for his enemies. It proved to be the most unique day in the annals of history. The centurion would have been unable to forget it.

But these remarkable facets of Jesus' behaviour and example would not, in themselves, have converted the centurion's soul. He required an understanding not only of Jesus' person but also of his work. That came in the same way as it did for the thieves. He heard the taunts of resolute unbelief.

Was Jesus of Nazareth the King of Israel, the Son of God? The priests denied it, poured scorn upon the idea, but how could the centurion explain the supernatural quality of Jesus' living and dying? Who was he? The question has never lost its fascination. Was he merely a Jewish martyr dying for his cause, or an impostor as the Sanhedrin claimed? Not far from where he was standing was the answer to the centurion's questions.

Earlier that day, he had supervised his men as they had hammered the 'accusation' above the heads of each of the victims. These had arrived directly from Pilate, the stamp of official Roman authority over the proceedings, and were therefore an important feature of each crucifixion. The 'accusation' appointed to be nailed to the central cross had met with Jewish disapproval. The Sanhedrin had sternly objected to the official wording, 'This is the King of the Jews', and insisted to the governor that it should be changed to 'He said, I am the King of the Jews' (John 19:19-21). But Pilate was adamant that the disturbing words must remain.

The centurion then, whose duties kept him near the crosses, was confronted for hours with the bold lettering, 'THIS IS THE KING OF THE JEWS'. It was written in three languages, Hebrew, Greek and Latin, the Roman's mother-tongue. There was no way in which he could escape from its challenging testimony. Even had he endeavoured to erase from his mind the marked impression Jesus had already made upon him, the wooden plaque with its simple message refused to pacify his conscience. The persistent question – Who is this man from Nazareth? – was repeated with the regularity of a drum beat. It was answered in wood.

The troubled pagan had surely by this time accepted, on the basis of having observed Jesus at close quarters, that he was a Jewish leader or even a king. He certainly did not appear regal. However, his noble bearing defied his humiliation, and blood-stained courage meant more to this veteran soldier than metaphysical abstractions. One matter could well have puzzled him, which earlier had bewildered Pilate. The governor had been impressed with Jesus, who in his lengthy conversation had graciously given Pilate every opportunity to believe in his claims (John 18:33-38). But Jesus did not look like a king, and, in any case, where was the evidence? Raw power was what impressed Roman conquerors. A manacled prisoner speaking about an unseen kingdom, which could not even boast an army, was not likely to be taken seriously. Yet there was 'something' about the Carpenter from Nazareth.

The 'evidence' was soon to arrive, but not in a way which the centurion would have expected. With the Lord of creation hanging limply on a tree, nobody should have been surprised if the realm of nature reflected the divine indignation. Having crept over the horizon, a very dark cloud edged its way towards Golgotha bringing with it hints of unruly weather to come.

When the Light of the world, in his final confrontation with the prince of darkness, was engulfed by its powers, something unusual was bound to happen. Although still only noon, a black cloak draped itself around skull hill and as far as the eye could see (Matthew 27:45).

The majority in Israel were not at the scene, yet they too experienced the impact of the Son of God's dying moments. The Father determined that nobody in Israel could turn his back upon history's greatest event, as torches were lit in every home and children scurried to safety in fear of the unknown. Across the land from Dan to Beersheba, from the Jordan to the west coast, nature must surely have responded to the cries of its Creator from the cross. Would not the animal kingdom have been silenced, the birds no longer singing, the oxen lowing or the sheep bleating?

The strange phenomenon gave rise to a great deal of speculation. Many would have remembered David's words in one of the messianic psalms, that God 'bowed the heavens also, and came down: and darkness was under his feet' (Psalm 18:9). The more learned probably brought the prophet Joel's words to mind, when almighty God revealed to him the cataclysmic events associated with the messianic hope: 'I will shew wonders in the heavens and in the earth, blood, and fire, and pillars of smoke. The sun shall be turned into darkness, and the moon into blood, before the great and the terrible day of the Lord come' (Joel 2:30,31).

In the meantime, as heavy mist hovered over Golgotha, everyone present at the site found himself trapped in the vortex of a mighty storm. The three victims, the priests, the Roman soldiers, John and his female companions—all experienced the terror of natural forces unleashed upon the scene. For three hours, from midday until mid-afternoon, the elements raged unrelentingly.

When they had begun the day, assigned to guarding and executing prisoners, the centurion and his men had no idea they had been called to engage in a battle. They were experienced at hand-to-hand combat, in blood-drenched skirmishes with fierce enemies seeking to kill them. They had no doubt scaled city walls, shielding themselves from arrows shot by expert bowmen, but the 'warfare' they met on skull hill was the toughest they had known.

Throughout the three hours, they were without respite from an 'enemy' they had no chance of defeating, against whom daggers and arrows were useless. What could Rome's imperial war machine do to defeat the wind which swept across the landscape? What Roman shield could shelter them from the 'arrows' of lightning which flashed towards them? How could military prowess grapple with 'hailstones and coals of fire' which flew from heaven? Even the centurion's commands to his men would be difficult to hear against a background of rolling thunder and shrill gusts, when 'the Highest gave his voice' (Psalm 18:13).

With no place to shelter, and desertion being unthinkable, the five soldiers drenched by the torrential rain gushing everywhere struggled to keep the crosses from falling in the gale. Three crosses, but only five men! The swirling winds and pounding hail fought back, as the soldiers wrestled with the weight of three helpless men pinioned to heavy wood. The task was made more difficult as the soldiers' sandals failed to grip the river of mud into which the crosses were erratically secured. It might have entered the centurion's mind that, with the power of the elements, how easily Jesus could have 'come down from the cross' if that had been his desire (Matthew 27:42)!

His three prisoners felt the full impact of the extraordinary situation. The shaking crosses chafed their wounded backs still further, the saturated twine tightened, biting deeply into cramped muscles, and the nails in Jesus' hands and feet tore angrily at his flesh. The anguished cries were pitiful to all but the most hardened observers. Blood-soaked sweat mingled with the rain, and ran in rivulets down their bodies, dropping from the feet to the miry ground.

The priests gathered their robes, slipping and sliding through the churned-up mud as they hastily escaped from the fury. Had the centurion known the psalm, the sight of Jesus' adversaries running as quickly as their long robes allowed would have caused him to remember the words: 'Let God arise, let his enemies be scattered:

let them also that hate him flee before him' (Psalm 68:1). The Roman would not have known the psalm, but he had by this time begun to appreciate the truth behind it. Part of his question had been answered. His prisoner from Nazareth was certainly a righteous man, whose cries to heaven were answered with authority and power (Psalm 18:6). It did not take long before the centurion received the solution to another aspect of his question.

Something even more remarkable happened, which convinced him that not only was Jesus a righteous man, but much more than that. The answer was provided as it became clear to everyone that Jesus' life was swiftly ebbing away. Near the cross, which was not as tall as artists have always depicted it, the centurion heard Jesus call to his 'Father': 'Father, into thy hands I commend my spirit'. It was the second time he invoked the name of 'Father' (Luke 23:34,46). The Roman was now assured of the relationship between Jesus and the Almighty behind the traumatic events.

Then, as everyone present watched, Jesus gathered what strength remained and cried out, 'IT IS FINISHED'! It was a plaintive yet triumphant shout of One who knew a great victory had been won. In the midst of a mighty storm, under the blackness of swollen clouds, the voice of Jesus pierced the gloom. There could be no doubting that the brief phrase had brought the life of Jesus to its close, and with it the unique and terrible day.

As Jesus' head slumped in death, the earth 'shook and trembled'. The spectators had endured three hours of terror, directed at them from above their heads. Now the ground shifted beneath their feet. Soon, the rumblings under the earth's crust grew to a crescendo with deafening results. The centurion had the answers he required: he knew Jesus of Nazareth was a righteous man, but now he believed with all his heart he was also the Son of God (Matthew 27:54).

With unseen and irresistible power the breath of almighty God cut a swathe from the hill to a nearby cemetery. Many graves were split wide open, and at the appointed time of Christ's resurrection God's people from the former days were miraculously liberated (Matthew 27:52,53).

3

THE INDIFFERENT SOLDIERS

*'Then the soldiers, when they had crucified Jesus, took
his garments, and made four parts, to every soldier
a part; and also his coat: now the coat was without
seam, woven from the top throughout'*
(John 19:23).

There were four of them, soldiers brutalized by the rigours of warfare and the hardships of life as a legionary in Caesar's army.
Only these experiences qualified them for the task of crucifying
their fellow men, one of the tasks allotted to the lower ranks.
Binding men to rough-hewn crosses, or even hammering metal
nails into flesh, were all part of a day's work for which their mea-
gre wages were paid. The invincible armies of Rome were not
expected to be squeamish about the sufferings of the conquered
races, nor of any one individual. Pity was not a quality admired by
Rome.

This had been evident earlier on, following the judicial scourging. Pilate, the Roman governor, had not ordered fresh cruelties to
be afflicted, but he did not object when his troops gratified their
bestiality upon their helpless and hapless victim. In fact, he probably expected it. It was one way the hardened legionary could be
kept in check under the harsh military discipline, to be permitted
his moments of lustful gratification.

They had cut Jesus down from the scourging trestle, and
watched him goaded by Roman daggers into the main building.
Out of sight of the crowds who had gathered to hear Pilate's judgment, even greater obscenities were enacted. The soldiers amused
themselves at Jesus' expense. With ruffian hands they ripped off
what was left of his clothing, until humiliated he stood naked
before the jeering onlookers. It says much for his physical strength

that he could endure the added punishments without collapsing under the strain.

Nearby there lay a soldier's scarlet mantle, a discarded one, for there was a great deal of blood on their victim's back and the owner would not have wanted his uniform soiled. It served a useful purpose as a regal robe, although not so impressive as Herod's had been a short while before. They draped it around Jesus' bruised and bloodied shoulders and, with a stick in his hand acting as a 'sceptre', the One who within weeks would be seated at almighty God's right hand in glory was pushed into his 'throne' by those who would bow before him. With a back and shoulders cut to ribbons by the scourging, the pain was excruciating.

Someone fetched a few twigs from a particularly thorny plant, and managed to twist it into the shape of a crown. The soldiers, more interested in fun than fashion, rammed it down upon Jesus' head until it was wedged and the skin was pierced. Fresh blood began to trickle, which promoted a frenzy of raucous delight. The King of an everlasting dominion, whom all other dominions will one day serve, suffered mockery from the lowly citizens of a decaying empire.

The Word of God who had become flesh, whose hand contains the iron rod of divine judgment, meekly submitted to the blows inflicted by hands covered in his own precious blood. Their foul spittle marked the face of him who holds the 'keys of hell and of death'. The prophecy of Isaiah was unknown to Jesus' tormentors, but he would have remembered it. 'I gave my back to the smiters, and my cheeks to them that plucked off the hair: I hid not my face from shame and spitting. For the Lord God will help me; therefore shall not I be confounded: therefore have I set my face like a flint, and I know that I shall not be ashamed. He is near that justifieth me; who will contend with me? let us stand together: who is mine adversary? let him come near to me' (Isaiah 50:6-8).

Whether the soldiers at Calvary had taken part in the charade is uncertain, but there is no reason why they should have been absent, as their duties involved being close to Jesus. So close, in fact, that within a few feet of his cross they squatted on the ground and sorted out his clothing among themselves.

It was one of the perks of the job that, having crucified their victims, those who had carried out the unenviable task were given first choice over which items of his few remaining possessions they wished to keep. They did not bother to wait until the owner was dead, but obscenely discussed the matter with each other against the background of his agonized groans.

For centuries, artists out of respect for their subject have depicted the crucified Christ wearing a loincloth. In fact he would have been naked. No objections were made by his mother and her companions at the loss of his dignity, and certainly not by the soldiers. A slave has no say in the matter, not being in the position to raise an objection. Instead, slavery presupposes submission to the whims and wishes of those who are its masters. A slave has no possessions he can call his own. Even the loincloth Jesus wore at the supper, as he bathed his disciples' feet, was a towel which belonged to the owner of the house.

The Son of God's abnegation was total. He surrendered himself fully as a slave to minister to sinners. Before Jewish contempt and abuse Jesus 'reviled not again', and at the mercy of Roman brutality 'he gave no answer'. Under the scourging he submitted without reservation, and when led to Golgotha was 'as a lamb to the slaughter'. He had given himself without reserve. All that remained was his fervent love for the Father, a nobility in suffering unmatched by any other, and a pitiful compassion even for the four throwing dice for his clothes.

Jesus had been aware of the predicament from childhood. He had known the messianic Psalm 22 by heart. What more significant place to recite its graphic poetry within the secret recesses of his soul, than when hanging from the tree destined for him? Jesus, devoid of self-interest ('I am poured out like water'), his body twisted in its agony ('all my bones are out of joint'), in possession of a broken heart ('my heart is like wax, it is melted in the midst of my bowels') and drained of all strength ('my strength is dried up'), recognized he was the subject of prophetic fulfilment.

In one of the tragic ironies of history, all that was taking place within a short space of men whose major concern was for second-hand clothing! The prophet Jeremiah expressed the pathos in a beautiful lament: 'Is it nothing to you, all ye that pass by? behold, and see if there be any sorrow like unto my sorrow, which is done unto me, wherewith the Lord hath afflicted me in the day of his fierce anger' (Lamentations 1:12). As if fulfilling the prophecy, the soldiers showed no pity for their victim. He prayed for their forgiveness, and in return they mockingly offered him vinegar. They cared for his clothes, but not for their souls. They had no idea that close by was One bearing the blazing wrath of divine and eternal displeasure on behalf of sinners like them.

His torment produced great anguish: 'I am a worm, and no man; a reproach of men, and despised of the people.' But the soldiers saw nothing attractive about what he was doing, only in what he had been wearing. Still, they undoubtedly heard the obscene laughter, abusive words and the blasphemy which would have hurt him much more: 'He trusted on the Lord that he would deliver him: let him deliver him, seeing he delighted in him.' It was the vindication of the voice of prophecy.

His was a desolation unequalled by any other experience known outside of hell itself ('Be not far from me; for trouble is near; for there is none to help'), without even the consolation of paternal comfort ('My God, my God, why hast thou forsaken me?'). He was the Master making atonement for his subjects, the Slave ministering to the enslaved. Yet hardly a soul in the entire world knew it!

As vultures pick for a long time over a carcass, the soldiers seemed unusually interested in the clothing. John, standing not far away, noticed 'they took his garments, and made four parts, to every soldier a part'. We know then there were four on duty, apart from the centurion, and their attention was drawn to Jesus' robe, headgear, sandals and belt: 'to every soldier a part'.

But there was a fifth item, his inner garment, which particularly fascinated them. John was no stranger to the 'coat', having been with Jesus for years, and was evidently interested to observe what would happen to it. In his Gospel he gives it a special mention.

The soldiers were unable to divide it among themselves into four separate parts, because it 'was without seam, woven from the top throughout'. Pity to spoil it! They therefore decided to cast dice for it. From the interest the soldiers took in this particular item of clothing, it would appear that the new owner would have considered himself 'fortunate' to have left the hill with his prized possession flung over his shoulder. But why were they so fascinated by Jesus' clothing, and particularly this one item? The answer lay in one particular part of it.

They considered it important that whoever won it from the four of them should possess the entire garment and not just a share of it. The fact was that this 'coat' had become almost as famous as its Owner. At least its hem had!

In the law, God had commanded that this part of the clothing had to possess a fringe, upon which would be a blue border. The purpose behind it was that the wearer would be continually reminded of 'all the commandments of the Lord, and do them' (Numbers 15:38,39). Jesus, who came to fulfil the law, was no exception. Upon the base of his inner garment was the blue border. It was this hem, looked at with pagan eyes, which claimed the attention of the Roman soldiers and was the reason why they felt it important that it should be kept intact.

Sadly, the hem, far from reminding most of the wearers of its original intention, namely the remembrance of the law's righteous demands, had instead become a superstitious talisman. Consequently, with Jesus' fame rippling further afield like the after-effects of a stone tossed into a pond, there arose a general desire among the weak and desperately needy to touch the blue border which encircled the base of his clothing. The belief was that personal benefits would be received by merely touching it; such was Jesus' reputation among the ordinary people for the purity of his life.

A very anxious and sick woman appears to have been the first to attract attention to the hem of Jesus' clothing (Matthew 9:20-22). She suffered from 'an issue of blood', which according to the law registered her as 'unclean'. The law emphasized the holiness of God; the strictures therefore upon her were severe. Menstruation was considered 'unclean', and a woman was separated for a week during her monthly cycle.

The sick woman had been suffering the penalty of separation for twelve long years. She was desperate, unable to tolerate her situation any longer. She had pushed through the crowds until she was behind Jesus, and then must have fallen to the ground before clasping the hem in the belief that by doing so she would be healed.

The touching of the hem appeared to be the reason for her healing, and at first perhaps to the woman herself, while in actual fact Jesus commended her faith. It was that simple, yet God-given gift of faith, which produced the divine response.

From that moving and compassionate moment, the superstitious belief spread that the mere touching of Jesus' clothing would automatically prove beneficial.

In the light, therefore, of the fame surrounding the border of blue on the Lord's clothing, it is small wonder the legionaries diced to possess it. Being superstitious, one can understand why they refused to damage the garment. They probably felt that the more of the hem they possessed, the greater its powers were.

How disappointed the soldier would have been, when at the end of the day he took his fancied prize back to the barracks, or at some later date to Rome! He could have boasted to his friends and relatives that he held in his hands the actual clothing worn by the famous Prophet, which possessed magical qualities. But when he attempted to show off its powers, they quickly discovered that what he had won in the lottery was not 'magic', but only second-hand cloth!

Poor men! Had they been less callous, and more attentive to the One whose clothing they coveted, these Romans would have heard a whispered prayer on their helpless behalf: 'Father, forgive them; for they know not what they do' (Luke 23:34). Such forgiveness was far more precious than any souvenir, and guaranteed to last much longer.

4

THE VENGEFUL PRIESTS

' . . . the chief priests mocking him, with the scribes and
elders, said, He saved others; himself he cannot save.
If he be the King of Israel, let him now come down from
the cross, and we will believe him. . . . He trusted in God;
let him deliver him now, if he will have him:
for he said, I am the Son of God.'
(Matthew 27:41-43).

The previous Sunday, the crowds had waved palms and had chanted their praises as Jesus entered Jerusalem seated on a colt of an ass. He had not done anything to undermine his popularity, yet by early morning on the following Friday the same excited people had been transformed into a seething and hateful mob demanding his death. It was an astonishing turnabout. The Sanhedrin, Israel's religious parliament, was responsible for it. The people were unaware that arrangements had been made by this fearsome body of priests to redirect their loyalties.

There were about 6,000 Pharisees in Israel, apart from the Sadducees and scribes. Most of them lived in the Jerusalem-Jericho regions. It was therefore a simple matter for the council to imprint its authoritative weight upon the priests as a whole, who in turn persuaded the people where their sympathies were to lie.

The Sanhedrin had the power of excommunication from the synagogue. Therefore, as many priests as could muster made their presence felt in the crowds who gathered to hear Pilate's judgment. Under pressure, they chose Barabbas instead of Jesus, and found themselves shouting 'crucify' as eagerly as they had once sung 'hosanna'.

Later the same day, some of the leading clerics appeared unexpectedly at Calvary, perhaps from among those who passed by mocking from a safe distance. They had no intention of remaining silent or aloof. This was their final opportunity for giving vent to their hatred for Jesus, a loathing born out of three years of intense rivalry and frustration. The fact that it was not customary for priests to be present at Roman executions only served to underline the determination of the council to rid itself of Jesus of Nazareth once and for all.

Through exhausted eyes, he observed their belligerent behaviour a few feet from him and remembered the prophetic words of the psalmist: 'They gaped upon me with their mouths, as a ravening and a roaring lion' (Psalm 22:13). He, like John the Baptist before him, had called them 'vipers' to their faces. Men who led the people in prayer, now encouraged them to curse, and the 'holy hands' of adoration had become the fists of 'wrath and doubting' (1 Timothy 2:8). It was not surprising. Jesus had openly called them hypocrites on more than one occasion.

Their prey was apparently cornered and, lacking the wisdom of Gamaliel (Acts 5:34-39), they wasted no time in trampling upon his teaching as if a few moments of mockery could undo his hitherto triumphant ministry. Any semblance of dignity their robes might have guaranteed them was compromised by such disgraceful behaviour as must have astonished even the Romans. Mocking the dying was a pastime few pagans engaged in, unless influenced by others who should have known better.

The merciless injustice, which had begun in the courtroom the previous evening, continued in a plethora of mocking provocation. Upon being challenged in front of Caiaphas about whether he was the Son of God, Jesus had astonished everyone by referring to himself as Daniel's glorious 'Son of man' (Daniel 7:13,14) to whom absolute power has been given (Matthew 26:63,64). It was for this, more than anything else, that the Sanhedrin desired Jesus' death.

To its members, he was a notorious blasphemer. Through false witnesses they had also charged him with wanting to destroy Jerusalem's Temple, and then claiming he could rebuild it within three days. They considered their prisoner to be a dangerous apostate in opposition to the traditional Jewish religion. Apart from the twelve apostles, he had even established his own 'sanhedrin' (Luke 10:1)!

Behind each taunt, though, lay a short fuse, ignited by Jesus' remarkable ministry, which had led to the continual explosions heard within the council chambers of the Sanhedrin and throughout the country. Very quickly, Jesus' fame and reputation had spread widely. The priests were envious. His popular appeal highlighted the people's mistrust of their religious leaders, his authority underlining their lack of it (Matthew 7:29).

Recognition of Jesus' claims had not taken long to rise to the surface, as Nathanael could have told the priests. Once he had met the Lord, he found no difficulty in accepting him as 'the Son of God . . . the King of Israel' (John 1:49). Mary of Magdala on the other hand, standing near them as they shouted at her Saviour, was a prime example of the fact that he had 'saved others'. Jesus having removed seven devils from her, she knew how much she owed him.

Reasoned argument, however, had never been the priests' strong point in their many confrontations with Jesus. At the cross only uncontrolled bigotry remained. Their violation of God's holy law, and general vindictiveness towards his Son, emphasized the truth that religious darkness is at its most intense when claiming to be light.

In one of a series of parables he related to the Temple authorities on the Monday before his crucifixion, Jesus summed up the national malaise. It was a simple tale; yet such was its impact upon the listeners that 'they sought to lay hands on him'. The only reason why they resisted was because they were fearful of a general uprising; such was the belief the crowds had in Jesus at that time.

The story concerned one who had been extremely busy in creating a vineyard, which involved the necessary preparation of planting, hedging and digging. He also had a tower built, so that his valuable property could be adequately watched over and protected. Then, when the work had been complete, he left the area to travel far, leaving everything in the hands of his employees that they might care for his vineyard during his absence.

However, once harvest time arrived the owner sent his servants to collect his due; but the employees refused to comply with his wishes and instead attacked the servants with sticks and stones, killing one of them. More servants were sent, but they were treated in the same way. Eventually, the owner sent his son in the belief that the employees would refrain from such violence, but to no avail. They also killed him, desiring to seize his inheritance (Matthew 21:33-46).

The priests understood the implied rebuke, recognizing the scriptural metaphor Jesus had employed.

Jesus presented the priests with a direct challenge which demanded a reply: when the lord in the parable returned, what would they expect him to do? There was only one obvious answer: 'He will miserably destroy those wicked men', and then they found themselves adding (no doubt against their wishes) 'and will let out his vineyard unto other husbandmen, which shall render him the fruits in their seasons.' With this admission, a gap opened up in their obduracy through which Jesus rode the coach and horses of his controversial reply.

He confronted them first of all with the fact of his ultimate and eternal authority, a truth rooted in one of the messianic psalms which would have been very familiar to them (Psalm 118:22,23). For the three years of his ministry among these 'builders' of Israel's house they had deliberately rejected the one stone which mattered in its construction, the chief corner-stone.

Had not God promised he would one day 'lay in Zion for a foundation a stone, a tried stone, a precious corner stone, a sure foundation' (Isaiah 28:16)? Jesus was that tried, precious and sure foundation, but the priests who stood before him and the many they represented had openly rejected him and his claims. As a result Judaism, like any other house without its chief corner-stone, would collapse.

The suggestion had enraged his audience, but to their dismay Jesus had more to say: 'And whosoever shall fall on this stone shall be broken: but on whomsoever it shall fall, it will grind him to powder' (Matthew 21:44).

The fury of Jesus' listeners at what appeared to them such a blasphemous remark had placed him in danger of physical abuse, like the son in the parable at the hands of the wicked employees. But Jesus continued to make a final point, one which underlined his 'heretical' teaching as far as the Sanhedrin was concerned: 'Therefore, I say unto you, The kingdom of God shall be taken from you, and given to a nation bringing forth the fruits thereof '.

The suggestion that such a notion was feasible, that God would remove the light of his countenance from Israel and favour the uncircumcised and hated Gentiles was tantamount to an admission of his heretical views.

In the light of this continuous debate between Jesus and the priests, which lasted the entire stretch of his ministry, how delighted the priests were when at last he was arrested and under their control. They were determined to witness his execution. Unable to walk away, or to reply to their maliciousness, Jesus suffered further humiliation as he hung in front of them weak and bleeding.

The raging reached fever pitch, as several years of enmity erupted in the intensity of a few moments. Men whose business it was to encourage religious belief, 'to do justly, and to love mercy, and to walk humbly' with their God, now found themselves the tools of Satan's vile intentions (Micah 6:8).

As for most to this day, the ungodly priests found the cross and the Christ upon it either a 'stumbling block' or just foolishness. Had they known the truth, far from leering at the Saviour's inability to descend from it, they would have recognized and rejoiced in his need to remain where he was.

Gradually, the abusive behaviour ceased as each of the priests in turn became aware that something unusual had happened. It was only midday, but the sun had disappeared behind a black cloud which had spread itself surreptitiously over the area like a cold hand, moving slowly onwards until the entire land was enshrouded. There were also indications of the storm which would later bombard the scene, with a cool breeze wafting across the hill, bringing with it flecks of rain and hail.

The bewildered spectators were more accustomed to the heat of a dry day, but their initial surprise quickly turned to astonishment. It was not long before thunder was heard in the distance, rolling towards Golgotha, and lightning flashed intermittently. The rain burst from the blackened sky in torrents. This was quickly followed by hailstones peppering them all, whipped up into a frenzy by the breezes which by this time had turned into cold wild winds.

There was no shelter from the storm. The soldiers were on duty and dared not leave their posts, and the little group at the foot of Jesus' cross refused to forsake their Lord at such a time. One could not imagine the priests remaining. Instead, saturated, they gathered their long robes around them and slithered through the mud as they sought to escape from the scene.

Thunder and lightning by this time directly overhead, and the sounds of rumbling beneath their feet, encouraged them in their haste. Had they thought about it, Psalms 18 and 22 might have sprung to mind. Heaven had noted their wickedness, had heard their taunts, and was reacting. But the priests little realized that there were more shocks awaiting them.

Upon reaching the city, no doubt trembling from fear, they discovered general consternation. Darkness overshadowed Jerusalem where there should have been daylight, and the noisy elements had driven the people into their homes for shelter. They were not there for long. Some time later, the shuddering earth told its own story, as the houses quickly emptied and the narrow streets filled with the sounds of confusion and panic.

Amidst the chaos, a rumour was heard. The priests would not have wanted to believe it. Apparently, deep inside the Temple the sacred veil made of intricately woven blue, purple and scarlet embroidery had been torn in two. But that was not all. The story circulated that the damage had not been afflicted by any human agency! Such a rich material could not have been ripped by hand, not even with a knife. Nevertheless, it had been torn 'from the top to the bottom' (Matthew 27:51).

The veil was a precious item in the house of God. It separated the most holy place from the eyes of sinners, lest they should see the area where almighty God chose to meet with his people. In the tabernacle during the Hebrews' journey in the wilderness, behind the veil had stood the ark of the covenant, the sacred symbol of his presence.

In the sixth century before Christ, the Babylonian armies captured the ark when they razed the Temple to the ground. Since then the most holy place, although vacant, was still a sacred spot where only the high priest could tread. He did so annually on the great day of atonement.

The rumour that the area was open to public view was a matter which greatly disturbed everyone. Apart from the high priests, nobody had dared contemplate the possibility of seeing beyond the veil. They would have remembered the scriptural example of Aaron's two priestly sons who offered 'strange fire' to God (Leviticus 10:1,2). That had taken place on the correct side of the curtain where the ordinary priests carried out their duties, yet Nadab and Abihu had been struck down by God and died on the spot.

With the news, Jerusalem's citizens had even more to concern them. Already God's anger was reflected in the elements, but what would happen to them now that the most holy place had been violated and could be seen by anyone?

The biblical story was of greater significance to the priests, many of whom had just returned from Calvary where their shameful behaviour had openly belied their profession. Caiaphas, together with representatives of the Sanhedrin, would undoubtedly have hurried to the Temple to see for themselves whether the report was correct. The shock upon realizing the truth was immense. It was the gravest crisis the council had faced, demanding an emergency sitting.

The high priest, although a Sadducee and not noted for his godliness, would nevertheless have been extremely anxious. He was a Roman appointee, and the Temple had been built by Herod in honour of the Caesar. Caiaphas was ultimately responsible for what took place within its spacious precincts, which were still in the process of completion. His fear of Rome overruled any reverence he might have had for God, despite the storm which at that moment held Jerusalem in its grip.

What had caused the damage? It was obvious to everyone it was not the work of vandals. The task would have proved too difficult. Besides, the Temple guards were especially concerned with the protection of so sacred an area as the 'holiest of all'. That left one conclusion, which the Sanhedrin was not prepared to contemplate, but it confronted the members with a dilemma for which there appeared no solution. When they issued their report, what were they to admit? Even if they believed it, Israel's religious leaders were not prepared to confess that God had brought judgment upon them all! It was clear, perhaps to them as well, that the events at Calvary had produced this situation.

There was another question. What was to be done in the immediate future? A practical problem required solving. The veil needed urgent repair, but this would mean the closure of that section of the Temple until another curtain could replace it. The most holy place was the focal point of daily worship, especially during the feast days; yet, with the secret place exposed, what would be the people's reaction? The chief priests and scribes had a great deal to discuss.

There was a greater problem which alarmed them. It was implied in the warning to Aaron the first high priest, that 'he come not at all times into the holy place' (Leviticus 16:2). Just once a year, and a unique privilege. Even someone as eminent in God's sight as Aaron had to tread carefully. His disobedience would have resulted in God's displeasure and his servant's execution. If Israel's high priest was under such an obligation, how would the most insignificant citizen fare now that he was able to see into the area where only high priests had once walked?

The truth was that nothing appeared to have happened to the person who had first reported the incident! Whoever he was (presumably a Temple guard), there is no record of his sudden death within the house of God. The divine anger had been withheld. Why was that? The members of the council refused to accept the logic behind this fact, but fair minds recognized that a miracle had taken place. It was God, exercising his great power through an earthquake, who had destroyed the separating veil. Later they discovered that the incident had occurred at the very moment of Jesus' death.

A new era had begun. Three years before, John the Baptist had preached about it: 'the axe is laid unto the root of the trees' (Luke 3:9). The 'axe' was in that same hand, and it was directed not at the twigs but at the roots of the tree: Judaism. In Christ, the old dispensation had given way to the new. The laws, rites and ceremonies so much an integral part of Israel had all been fulfilled in him, God's only begotten Son. He was the One, to the nation's shame and embarrassment, whom its leaders had mocked and reviled and 'crucified and slain'.

There was an irony about the priests' behaviour. Watching Jesus in the throes of death, the Sanhedrin assumed it could officially record the end of his troublesome influence. Quite the reverse. It was the fabric of the Jewish religious system, represented by Jerusalem's council, which was dying. Formal observance, even cold servility, to the minutiae of numerous traditions had been swept to one side by 'a new and living way'. In his Son, God had bypassed the ruling body of Judaism, and was about to bring to birth a 'royal priesthood' (1 Peter 2:9).

Unlike the Pharisees, Sadducees and scribes, this 'kingdom of priests' rejoices in the removal of legalism's 'heavy burden'. Instead, as a body accepted in his Son and heeding the King's command, it marches boldly towards the 'ark', with his Law written in its heart by free and sovereign grace (Ezekiel 36:26,27).

Like the jewels in Aaron's breastplate, the names of the royal members of this priesthood have been worn on the eternal high priest's heart at the bar of judgment. As a consequence, nothing can remove their right of access to heaven's 'holiest of all', or hinder their progress towards it.

The priests that Jesus knew were, like most sinners in religious circles, endeavouring to affect a holiness which had no bearing upon reality. Jesus exposed the hypocrisy, charging them with being like a cemetery, 'beautiful outward, but . . . within full of dead men's bones' (Matthew 23:27).

The royal priesthood is much different. It is continually being washed in the purest of 'water', the precious blood of Christ (1 Peter 1:18,19). It is also dressed in the finest of robes befitting its high rank, not to impress others as Israel's priests did, but rather to reflect the purity of the great high priest. The 'uniform' is that of imputed righteousness, 'fine linen, white and clean', one not bought or earned but provided by the King himself (Revelation 19:14).

Then again the 'holy nation' is a standard-bearer for revealed truth, as well as its custodian, and its citizens seek to emulate their Lord's example in his submission to its precepts. They do not add to God's Word the traditions of men, as those who mocked Jesus had done, nor do they disbelieve the prophets' messages and yet 'garnish' their tombs for effect. In the new era, heralded by John the Baptist and introduced by God's own Son, the citizens of the new Israel 'hear the word of God, and keep it' (Luke 11:28).

However, these truths were unknown to the members of the council. They had more practical matters to concern them. It was to prove a busy weekend. As they considered what was to be done about the damage in the Temple, more astonishing events occurred in the city. Within three days of the darkness which over-shadowed Jerusalem, and the gigantic storm which accompanied it, another and more astounding rumour was heard. Just beyond the city wall the earth had shaken violently, and the body of Jesus of Nazareth was missing from its tomb!

5

THE THIEF:
REACHING FOR THE LIGHT

'Lord, remember me when thou comest
into thy kingdom'
(Luke 23:42).

Golgotha had witnessed many crucifixions, the path to skull hill being well worn by the imprints of distressed men goaded to their execution. It was always a pathetic parade of those without hope, and for whom there was no return. The sweltering heat, the sweat, the harshness, the grime and the groans: these were the familiar features of such occasions.

However, when Jesus trod the same pathway, remarkable events occurred. Not least was that which concerned the transformation in one of the thieves who accompanied him. Within hours his bitter aggression, typical of prisoners in his position, had given way to an unusual meekness of spirit when one considers his situation. Hope had been substituted for despair, joy for desperation. The change in the man was so remarkable, and those at the scene so astonished by what they saw, that to the present day his experience is quoted. It was an example of what God can do in the final few moments of a wasted life.

The man's arrival at the dreadful place undoubtedly began the process. His arrest, imprisonment, even the brutal scourging – nothing he had experienced or endured in his life could be compared with the prospect of his being crucified. Those who travelled the lonely route to skull hill were usually too bruised, and suffering too much pain, to be able to think about what lay ahead of them. Rancour, and the spirit of bravado in front of the milling crowds, were what most quelled their fears. It was just as well.

But it could not last long. The quizzical bystanders grew fewer as the procession passed through the city gate, and made its tortuous way to the hill. To the victim, this must have been the first moment when the reality of his impending death gripped his mind. He realized he could no longer claim to have a recognized place in society, the normal processes of life having given way to a continuous nightmare. The victim would have wanted the clock to have been turned back, to escape down the hill into the anonymity of Jerusalem's streets: anything but the inevitability of his agonizing death.

The thief was no different from others of his kind. Reaching the plateau, he fell exhausted to his knees and gained his first sight of Golgotha. The end of the road! Unmerciful soldiers, sturdy timber, rope, twine, a hammer and some nails were nearby – the accoutrements required for the day's events. It was more than sufficient to cause the thief to panic. He clutched the 'straw' nearest to him, the knowledge that Jesus of Nazareth claimed supernatural powers.

It was the only hope the desperate man possessed. With his friend, he continued shouting to Jesus to exercise his authority and enable them to escape even after the crosses had been raised into position. There was no practical response. Instead, he heard a prayer!

Soon afterwards, the power he sought descended upon Calvary. It began slowly. The morning had been so full of activity, few would have noticed the appearance on the horizon of the smallest of dark clouds. With the erection of the crosses, the priests chanted their hatred and the soldiers diced for clothing; and the cloud gradually spread widely until it appeared to wrap itself around the sun. In place of the glare of light normally experienced at that time of day, an eerie gloom settled over the area like a blanket drawn by an unseen hand. Then it moved onwards until it covered the entire land.

A few spots of rain danced on the thief's forehead, and these were quickly followed by a deluge, bringing welcomed relief to his fevered brow. It was short-lived. Soon, skull hill appeared to quiver as the persistent crack of thunder exploded directly overhead, and lightning frequently lit the scene as it raced through the clouds. The thief had never known such fear. He saw the priests scurrying through the mud, but there was nowhere he could go. Hailstones pounded his naked body, winds howled around his cross shaking at the mercy of an earthquake. One of the legionaries struggled to keep the cross in its position.

The thief was ignorant of the messianic psalm, which provided a warning a thousand years in advance of what was to be expected when the Messiah was surrounded by 'the sorrows of death'. However, it made no difference. Terror is not more comfortable to endure when it is expected. Still the thief, incapable of escaping from the centre of the phenomena, was in no doubt Who was behind it.

As Calvary witnessed the brunt of divine wrath revealed through nature, like Titans clashing, he was confronted with the God of creation in his awesome power. For the sovereign Creator, no force is irresistible or object immovable. Nothing anywhere in his universe can prevent the fulfilment of his purposes, no man hinder or deter his decrees. The realization stirred the thief to act upon it.

With as much energy as he could muster, he shouted earnestly to his fellow thief on the other side of Jesus. Did he not fear God? There was no response. Perhaps he sought consolation from one with whom he could identify, but the attitude he saw reflected in his comrade only made him more alarmed.

The agonies of crucifixion, the furious weather, the hopelessness of their position: these should surely stimulate a fear of the Creator. But no interest was shown, or any comforting words from his friend. He should have realized that those without hope cannot provide it for others. The truth must have suddenly dawned upon him, that in the most extreme of circumstances the world is bereft of comfort. He was alone, adrift in a friendless environment.

Like all ungodly men, he had probably always attributed his secret apprehensions under an angry sky to the immaturities of youth or the superstitions of the simple. However, admitted or not, the elements are capable of causing the strongest to weaken and the most arrogant to tremble. When at the centre of a storm, even the disciples, who were professional fishermen and expert seamen on Galilee's lake, were panic-stricken and cried out to Jesus for help.

But not all the fearful turn to God, or even acknowledge him. The other thief was a prime example. It is one thing to tremble underneath the weight of a storm, and another to fear the majestic God whose power lies behind it. Only his grace, like a stretched-out arm from heaven, can do that. As with the apostle Peter, it was the unseen and gracious hand of the Father and not mere 'flesh and blood' which had touched the thief's heart (Matthew 16:17).

Like others that day at Calvary, he suddenly realized that the phenomenal occurrences were in some way connected with Jesus. How else could the strangeness of it all be explained? Had he been as close to the Son of God as the disciples, and for as long, he would have come to expect the unusual. Yet with the minimum of fuss and faith, enough to save him, he was enabled to grasp something of the significance of Christ, as his vital request to him implied.

When grace is given by the Spirit, the experience does not begin and end with the fear of God. The thief was heard to say much more to his villainous companion, an extraordinary statement which testified to the transformation in his life and character. He would have been justified as a dying man in sparing his words, but he felt compelled to recognize publicly his sinfulness and warn others of theirs. Far from seeking to escape from his tragic circumstances as he had done not long before, he admitted his guilt and that of the other thief. Their suffering and inevitable execution, he maintained, was just and in accordance to the law. They were receiving 'the due reward' for their sins. Such a confession, from one undergoing the extremities of a crucifixion, was truly amazing and could only be understood in terms of divine grace flooding his soul.

Evidently, a miracle as dynamic as the weather conditions had taken place within him. He was in the position in which God's law, applied by the Holy Spirit, places every sinner, as Paul reminds us: 'that every mouth may be stopped, and all the world may become guilty before God' (Romans 3:19). The thief's 'mouth' was shut; all arguments had ceased. He knew not only that he was a sinner (the entire world knows that!), but that sin controlled and dominated him because of his estrangement from God.

All attempts to justify himself in the sight of his righteous Creator had ended. He now saw for himself that throughout his life he had been 'in sin', a breaker of God's holy law, and therefore justly deserved the appropriate punishment. Whether a thief on the lowest rung of society, or an acclaimed Pharisee, the convicted sinner squirming under the holy gaze of the divinely given Commandments has no other desire but to hold his head in his hands and cry, 'O wretched man that I am! who shall deliver me from the body of this death?' (Romans 7:24).

It is at the end of one's tether that salvation is best realized, when the soul has been humbled and the rebellious spirit overcome. The thief felt the Spirit's compulsion to turn to his only hope of rescue. It was not from the cross he needed to escape, but from the eternal consequences of his sin. He had not known that truth when he first arrived at Golgotha.

The fear of divine power, and the recognition of his sin: these led him to the soul's safest resting place, the Son of God. He knew Jesus as 'this man', but Jesus' fame was such throughout Israel that both the thieves must have heard a great deal about him, albeit from a distance. Their kind had a secret regard for the unusual Carpenter of Galilee, who took the trouble to associate with the 'publicans and sinners', all of whom were social and religious outcasts. Jesus was very popular among them.

He was sympathetic towards these rejected people, if not to their sinful way of life, at least to their plight. Without excusing their behaviour, Jesus saw them as victims of the politico-religious system which had reared them. They all appreciated that he went out of his way to show them love and pity, to socialize with them and listen to their grievances. The apostle Peter later testified that Jesus 'went about doing good, and healing all that were oppressed of the devil; for God was with him'. Few would have denied the latter.

With the experience of being close to Jesus, the thief had the opportunity of seeing at first hand the nobility of Jesus' character, the remarkable meekness in the face of aggressive opposition and his gracious submission to events. While others defied their 'fate' and cursed their 'luck', Jesus had revealed a patience in suffering so unique that it could not but be noticed by those whose manner betrayed their ungodliness.

Something else astonished the thief. In his dying moments, he and his friend stared out from their crosses and cursed. By contrast, Jesus gazed upwards towards heaven and prayed. To the thief, a stranger to God's throne, it appeared out of place in Golgotha's ungodliness. Yet, rather than aggravate his cynicism, the content of the prayer stirred him: 'Father, forgive them; for they know not what they do.'

It was a simple prayer, and its simplicity was what made it so compelling, and without doubt the most sublime moment in an otherwise grotesque experience. The thief's thoughts were plain: 'this man' had been scourged, reviled and mocked, and nails had been hammered into his hands and feet. But without seeking rescue from his plight, he forgave those responsible for his suffering! It is never an easy matter loving one's enemies, but how much more difficult when nailed by them to a tree! Anyone capable of such a prayer was in possession of a secret worth knowing.

The thief was now convinced in his own mind of Jesus' authenticity. There was an unusual quality to his character which could not be dismissed, a purity which fascinated the worldling. In making his plea to his friend he had to mention it: 'this man hath done nothing amiss'. It was the position to which only divine grace can bring a repenting sinner, the public recognition of the deity of Christ.

Within moments, the thief had been transformed from an antagonist to a fervent disciple of Christ. Without Jesus having said anything to him, the man no longer desired to revile the Saviour but found himself believing in him. In fact, he was not content with a silent affirmation of Jesus' claims, but overcame his weakened condition to make his belief known. Like Peter, his heart and soul united in a joyous acclamation: 'Thou art the Christ, the Son of the living God' (Matthew 16:16).

It was that recognition which enabled him to understand Jesus' prayerful reference to his Father. To whom was he speaking? The converted thief now understood. The 'Father' was the Being whose power lay behind the traumatic events that day: the darkness, the torrential rain, the hailstones, the howling winds and the earthquake. He possessed such awesome power, but is a 'Father'! In which case, reconciliation between him and sinners is possible. 'This man' had prayed, 'Father, forgive them'. There is hope, and the thief yearned to avail himself of it.

In one of the most moving passages recorded in Scripture, to which all those close by were witnesses, the dying thief appealed to the One he now knew to be the mysterious Messiah. No longer did he feel isolated in a grim situation, anticipating the darkness of an endless night. Now he possessed the only ingredients redemption recognizes, faith and hope coupled to Christ.

Much nearer 'midnight' than the 'eleventh' hour, there must have been anxious moments. Would Jesus hear his whisper? It may have been too late. Perhaps Jesus was already dead. There was no time to be lost. Satan was near. Heaven and hell vied with each other for the possession of the criminal's soul, and both loomed large over the scene. A mere gasp from eternity, he turned to Jesus and through swollen lips he whispered, 'Lord, remember me when thou comest into thy kingdom' (Luke 23:42).

Some have wondered where the thief heard the gospel. There can be no salvation without an understanding of the essential message. As Paul stated: 'How then shall they call on him in whom they have not believed? and how shall they believe in him of whom they have not heard? and how shall they hear without a preacher?' (Romans 10:14).

The thief would probably have come under the sound of the gospel as it filtered through the various strata of Jewish life, but there was a more reliable channel. Golgotha itself was the finest 'pulpit' in the land, where the truth about Jesus was uppermost in the minds of the observers even if it was not believed. The thief could not have failed to hear the message, for it was shouted, albeit irreverently, from several directions.

There were the pitiless priests. They led the chorus of shameful abuse: 'If he be the King of Israel, let him now come down from the cross, and we will believe him . . . He saved others; let him save himself, if he be Christ, the chosen of God.' From a distance, casual spectators echoed the unbelief, and then presumably walked away laughing among themselves.

The possibility of the new convert possessing some knowledge of Jewish belief, from the rabbinical teaching of his youth, was the reason why he did not require instant instruction about the finer points of what he was hearing. Although his understanding would have been poor, he grasped certain vital aspects of truth.

The first was that he desperately needed to be set free from his predicament. Not long before, he had struggled to escape from the horror of crucifixion and the certainty of death, but now he realized he was confronted by a far greater peril. He required delivering from the slavery which sin had brought to his soul. He had come to the end of his life, to the brink of an eternity stretching endlessly ahead of him, and God's ledger would record that all he had been in the sight of his Creator was a thief, a breaker of the divine holy law!

He was not confused by the display of unbelief, even from the priests, for mysteriously it had been revealed to him that imprisonment does not only consist of iron bars and locked doors, or of hands and feet fastened securely to a tree. Freedom is the ability prayerfully to forgive the tormentors, to turn the other bruised cheek graciously towards the enemy, and to refuse to revile the revilers. All these virtues the thief and everyone present had witnessed in Christ's behaviour. He was free, even in the process of crucifixion, but his accusers were imprisoned in the mesh of their evil ways.

The thief's knowledge of the Jewish scriptures would have been very limited, but through the revelation given to him he also now wholeheartedly believed that his only hope lay in the Son of God. His was a simple childlike faith, as small as a grain of mustard seed, but it enabled him to trust his Friend and Saviour implicitly.

If this man is King, then to him alone must petitions be made. The thief would no more have questioned him than he would have disobeyed Herod, or the centurion the emperor in Rome. O to be the citizen of a kingdom ruled over by such a King! The urgent and earnest request was made: 'Lord, remember me when thou comest into thy kingdom.'

From one who not long before had cursed his way to Calvary, and had shouted abusively at Jesus, came the humility of a truly repentant sinner. The thief, recognizing the depth of his unworthiness, wanted only to be remembered. A mere glance in his direction was all this piece of broken humanity believed he could expect when, as the long-awaited Messiah, he made his appearance with his triumphant armies at the close of the age.

Like all Jews, the new convert's view of the messianic hope, if it existed at all, was blurred. The approaching Kingdom, even if it had begun its journey, seemed over the brow of numerous distant horizons. However, true faith must be exercised or it does not exist. Like the elderly Abraham, after God had promised the birth of Isaac to him and the equally aged Sarah, the ex-thief 'against hope believed in hope' (Romans 4:18).

It is the paradox every true child of God confronts, and understands, when plain logic is superseded by spirituality and reason is obliged to bow to faith. The possibility of his being 'remembered' a millennium or more beyond his days by the divinely appointed Messiah appeared as hopeless as fatherhood to a man 'about an hundred years old'. But, like 'faithful Abraham', the newcomer to faith did not 'stagger' unbelievingly but trusted God implicitly.

This was a new experience for him, but clutching his simple faith he surrendered his soul to Christ for eternal safekeeping: 'Remember me'. Within those moving few seconds, frozen in time through the pages of Scripture, is encapsulated God's tender compassion for sinners.

With both their lives ebbing away, Jesus' reply was as startling as it was unexpected. Although he found it difficult to speak, he whispered back assuringly: 'To day shalt thou be with me in paradise.' Not in some vague distant future, but within a few moments! And he would not be merely remembered, but warmly welcomed and embraced. Today! Assurance of salvation is a blessed gift from God to his covenant people, but for the thief who expected nothing but a mere glance it proved a doxology to his soul.

He would not formerly have understood the word 'paradise' (the heavenly 'park'), but now he realized it was associated with Jesus. He had said 'with me'!

Within fleeting moments, the repentant thief's crumpled form would be dragged from the scene, but although he would be 'absent from the body' he would nevertheless be 'present with the Lord'. He had entered into the joy of his Saviour.

All that he had lost in Eden (1 Corinthians 15:22) he gained at Golgotha, exchanging ashes for beauty, mourning for joy and the spirit of heaviness for the garment of praise. No longer did he hear the cacophony created by the vicious and the vile. With his new-found Friend in paradise, he was introduced to the sounds of eternal adoration and the full glare of everlasting glory. Being with Christ is certainly 'far better'.

6

THE THIEF:
SINKING IN THE SHADOWS

*'Dost not thou fear God, seeing thou art
in the same condemnation?'*
(Luke 23:40).

There were eight men with Jesus in the procession that headed towards Calvary: Simon of Cyrene, the centurion, four soldiers and the two thieves. Little did they realize, but Jesus harboured a secret which, had they known about it, would have startled them. They would probably not have believed him. Even those in sympathy with Jesus would have found it remarkable.

Despite what appeared a situation devoid of hope, he knew that the compassionate hand of the Father was already laid upon three of the men. Like morning dew the silent refreshing influences of grace were already at work. It did not take long for the effects to be felt in their lives. Simon (and later his entire family), the centurion and the questing thief had all been brought to the foot of Christ's cross in more ways than one.

In discussions about what happened at Calvary the other thief is invariably overlooked, hidden away in the shadows cast by the cries of the Christ and the whispers of his compatriot in crime. Yet his must rank as one of the most tragic of all the stories told by history, the day he spent in the company of God's eternal Son and refused to believe it. Within feet of him, the gates of paradise opened wide and heavenly rejoicing over a repentant sinner rang out, but enshrouded in darkness he missed the moment. Instead, his tormented soul sank deeper into black mire.

The unrepentant thief, for no mention is made of any change in him taking place, would have heard about Jesus long before the day they met each other. Jesus' fame, as we have already noted, had been widespread throughout his three years ministering in Israel. With multitudes flocking to him each day to hear his teaching and receive his healing touch, there could not have been many households that had not come under Jesus' influence in one way or another. It could be argued that this man was no exception.

Still, the nearest he had got to Jesus was in the early morning of Good Friday. The cell block in Pilate's fortress of Antonia, where both the thieves would have been incarcerated, was a hive of gossip as each fresh prisoner brought the latest news with him. This time the chatter was about the well-known Jesus of Nazareth. The remarkable prophet and miracle worker had been arrested, and soon he would be joining them in the cells. The previous evening confirmed the rumour, for there had been much activity within Antonia and the sounds of marching outside, as a contingent of Roman soldiers had been involved in the arrest.

The cells were not intended to provide comfort for the prisoners; the thickness of the walls and the sturdiness of the bars were the only considerations. In the dank atmosphere, the prisoners possessed little hope and no possibility of escape. Their only occupation was to await their fate at the governor's discretion and dream of better times.

As the prisoner thought about his future, the sounds of the crowds not far away must have wafted towards him, for the 'pavement' (the vast area in front of the palace) would have been close by. He and his cell mates, including one notorious criminal called Barabbas, guessed what was happening. Not only had they heard of Jesus' arrest but occasionally the chanting of his name reverberated around the precincts. Soon the excitement arose in the cells. The prisoners, with their ears pressed against the bars, could detect another name being shouted. There was no mistaking it. The crowd shouted in unison, 'BARABBAS!'

They were all acquainted with the custom, although this time there was even more drama than usual attached to the occasion. Annually during the Passover feast, the governor released one of the prisoners as an act of public clemency. It may have proved merciful for the winner of this lottery, but not for the 'unlucky' ones like the thieves. Being brought so close to freedom increased the agony of their situation. Each prisoner spent the day, to the very moment of the governor's choice, in a state of agitation. The choice could not have been more stark. It was either a scourging and an agonizing death – or freedom. Even in that apparent act of mercy Roman cruelty was evident.

The prisoners now had no doubt who was the 'lucky' one among them. Crestfallen faces and embittered curses told their story. That year Barabbas, a thief, murderer and insurrectionist, was obviously the chosen one out of them all. The more they listened, the more confident they became that this was so.

But why this apparent arbitrary decision to release Barabbas? After all, he was much worse than any of them! They must surely have discussed the question among themselves. The discussion was not merely an academic one. Their lives had literally rested upon the decision Pilate had been forced to make at the insistence of the mob. Why had he not chosen one of them? When the thieves therefore were taken from their cells for the judicial scourging prior to the journey to Calvary, they were in a bitter mood. They had been close to freedom, only to have it snatched from their grasp at the very last moment.

The scourging, always the preliminary to crucifixion, served to make them even more embittered. Recognized as being an extremely brutal way of administering punishment, no Roman citizen was allowed by law to receive it. The victim was stripped to the waist and tied to the post in a bent position, so that his back was taut and well-exposed. Then two powerfully built men ('lictors') standing on either side of him delivered the blows in quick succession. Many strong men died as a result. Most would have fainted.

The 'lictors' carried whips with leather thongs, each one weighted with jagged edges of bone or lead, and as each blow was struck the pieces dug deeply into the flesh. Soon open wounds formed a network of rivulets across the back, and the blood oozed freely from them until it dripped from the flesh hanging like ribbons. At times when the sufferer twisted and flinched in agony, the thongs failed to find their target and instead curled over the shoulders or around the head.

There is no record of how many stripes were prescribed on Good Friday morning, but the customary number would have made it difficult for the victims to remain standing. Nevertheless, they were forced to summon up what energy remained for the agonizingly slow journey to skull hill.

Mention has already been made of a victim's first sight of Golgotha, as he passed through the city gates to his execution. It would have been enough to reduce even the most hardened of criminals to a state of extreme nervous tension. Everyone knew it was known as the place of a skull, a notorious area which prisoners visited only once. As he drew nearer the spot, and saw the trunk of thick wood laid out on the ground waiting for him and the crossbeam he carried, terror gripped him. There could have been few exceptions.

The thief reacted in a way expected of him. Overawed by the shadow cast over the area, with the gruesome spectre of death by crucifixion facing him, he was very frightened. Death was close at hand, not in the comforts of his own bed, but secured to a creaking gibbet. However ostentatiously he might have worn on his sleeve a light-hearted spirit, there was no doubting the fear now that his destination had been reached.

It resulted in him shouting obscenities, as desperate men do when in a hopeless situation. There were various targets to which his accusations could have been aimed. Represented in front of him was the hated Roman empire, whose occupational forces were detested by every Jew. It would have been understandable had he expressed his loathing for Rome, knowing he was beyond recrimination.

There were the chief priests, scribes and elders for whom the social outcasts had no respect, and whose hypocrisy had become a renowned aspect of Jewish life. Then again, he had cause to curse Pilate the governor who had arbitrarily chosen Barabbas instead of him. Even his 'bad luck' could have been an excuse for his angry outburst. However, he did not express his bitterness and frustration against any of them. Instead, he reviled Jesus!

The reason for this was plain. The taunting priests had provided both thieves with a ray of hope, a possibility of escape from the terror they knew they would shortly experience. In a public exhibition of inexcusable ungodliness, some of the leading members of the Sanhedrin began decrying Jesus' messianic claims. If he was Israel's King, the Son of God, all he had to do was to prove it by descending from the cross. The desperate men clutched the suggestion like drowning men a life raft.

It was probably at this point that the indifferent thief lost interest in Jesus, his personal safety being of greater importance to him than anything else. The frightened are likely to call selfishly upon God, not requesting mercy, but seeking rescue from their circumstances. Such was the thief's instinct. He had no intention of submitting to Jesus' claims upon him, but was merely using him as a talisman for his own ends. He did not really believe Jesus could help him, but it was worth a try: 'If thou be Christ, save thyself and us.' The fear of dying produced uneasy companions: blasphemous unbelief coupled to a plea for divine assistance!

But Jesus made no attempt to use the powers he claimed to possess, and to the thief that was failure. From that moment, his heart having hardened, the sun began to set upon any possibility of his sharing in the experience of his comrade. The unbeliever is only interested in a pragmatic view of religion, whether it works, and especially whether it works for him. In any case, the thief found comfort in the fact that the religious leaders evidently shared his opinion about Jesus.

Yet, the Father granted the rebel a final opportunity to acknowledge and revere him. He did so by intensifying the man's fear in the face of the extraordinary weather conditions, for which the first Good Friday was noted. Gradually, the unexpected twilight turned into the blackness of night and overshadowed him. Until then, the presence of his two companions had been a source of comfort to him; but now, although he heard their sighs and groans, he could no longer see them. It was a reminder to him of the 'outer darkness' which confronted him, where the isolation is total and the sounds are of an eternal 'weeping and gnashing of teeth'. It made no difference. Pride leapt high when submission was called for.

But still the Father had not finished with him. Even as he hung helplessly in the darkness, the rebellious sinner was lashed by powerful forces. Great gusts of wind swooped upon his cross, threatening to lift it from its socket, and driving the energetic rain into his face. As he sought to regain his breath, his naked body was lashed by myriads of hailstones, causing him to gasp still further. Claps of thunder appeared to shake heaven itself, and the earth was illuminated by numerous flashes of lightning – but the thief's heart remained as black as the occasion.

With each fresh onslaught, the proud and stubborn rebel endured everything his Creator blew upon him. He turned his thoughts heavenward and expressed his defiance to the sky. He was alarmed, even terrified, but he who had been a hardened villain in his life was determined not to weaken in his death.

His arms and legs were deeply lacerated by the twine, and his twisted body was distorted with pain. His lonely vigil was made even more distressing with the knowledge that if his death was long in coming his legs would be broken. The fresh agonies resulting from his helpless body resting upon them would bring death much closer.

But despite all this, he struggled to maintain his independence from God. He was resolved not to repent, and in doing so may have wondered why he was incapable of fearing the One who 'after he hath killed hath power to cast into hell' (Luke 12:5). It may have been because he had lived in sin for too long. Perhaps there had been a time years before when he might have found it a simple matter to reject his way of life. With the passing of the years, though, it had become steadily more difficult. Friendships had been formed not easily broken, sinful practices indulged in too enjoyable to lose. A sensitive conscience had become seared.

As a thief, he was a lawbreaker not only in society's eyes, but particularly in the eyes of God whose law it was. Thus, although he was in Christ's company for hours, instead of softening his heart, the experience served to harden it. Holiness has that effect upon others, because the heart's inclination is towards wickedness (Jeremiah 17:9).

But even so, God had not yet rejected him. As he clung to life in the shadows, the divine hand touched his conscience. It was a kind Providence which ordained that a common criminal should share his dying moments with his only Son, and at a time when he was urgently required. Golgotha would have been a more bleak and friendless place without him!

For hours he was within touching distance of the Messiah, whose awesome purity surely pierced the dark recesses of the thief's soul. Even his friend had shouted across to him what had been evident to everyone who had heard of Jesus, namely, that he had 'done nothing amiss'. He saw the gracious demeanour under extreme provocation as clearly as everyone else, and recognized the compassionate and selfless spirit flowing through the gentle prayers. Yet, without understanding why, he knew that for no apparent reason his quarrel was with Jesus.

His situation was not conducive to self-examination, but one question might have presented itself in some obscure recess of his mind. Apart from the bitterness of his disappointment at having his request for rescue denied, why was he so antagonistic to this virtual stranger from Nazareth? It is the dilemma confronting every sinner. Justice and fairness insist that Jesus 'went about doing good'. Why then oppose him?

It was not the priests' unseemly mockery and the passing spectators' taunting cruelty which angered the sinner. Rather, it was the obvious innocence and purity of his companion on the next cross. The thief found within himself a loathing for Jesus which he would not have been able to fathom. There is a fellowship in darkness as well as in light. Had it registered in his heart, he would have realized that this strange contradiction pointed to the truth of Jesus' claims. He is God, the Light exposing sin, a fact which no sinner can tolerate (John 7:7).

There was something else. The Father also reminded him of the divine message, to which the Son had testified. There was no doubting it. A torrent of verbal abuse was aimed at Jesus by the priests, but in the display of bigoted intolerance certain fundamental truths could be heard ringing out clearly as if refusing to be smothered by the prevailing unbelief. They were like pieces of gold on black velvet. The ungodly found themselves proclaiming the truth, albeit through clenched teeth: Jesus' example was that he trusted God, his mission was to save sinners and his calling was that of Israel's King-Messiah. In fact, he was none other than the Son of God!

The unbeliever was being given a last opportunity to accept the truth, and there was no doubt that he understood what was expected of him. Nobody needed to explain to him the meaning behind the word 'Christ' when he called out to him, 'If thou be Christ . . .'. He understood as all Jews did, for the rabbis would have taught him in his youth, that the word 'Messiah' was eternally linked with the divine intention of redeeming his people. Even the adulterous Samaritan woman appreciated that. In short, what more could God's love have done to impress him of his need of redemption and reconciliation?

But it was to no avail, the heart being 'deceitful above all things and desperately wicked'. Nothing the hardened sinner had heard Jesus say had the slightest effect upon him. Cynicism ('IF thou be Christ . . .') had taken over where fear had formerly held sway. He heard Jesus' prayer and his request that his enemies should be forgiven, but the loving gesture made no difference to him. After all, he was desperate to be rescued and had pleaded with Jesus to use his messianic powers, but nothing had happened. Prayer not having appeared to work for him, the cynic wants to know what useful purpose it has.

He heard the whispered conversation with its promise of paradise, but cynicism is not impressed by those like his former friend who covet divine help only when death is beckoning. The cynic despises men for less than that. Besides, he was more concerned about the tangible pleasures of this life than any benefits he might receive in an invisible paradise about which he knew nothing. Not only was this rebel refusing to repent before God, whom he was shortly to confront, he was also rapidly losing his ability to do so.

In the only use God made of him, he is a symbol until the end of time of the horrendous nature of man's fall. God promised the first parents 'death' if they wilfully disobeyed him. They did, and as a consequence were driven from his presence and fellowship. Cherubim guarded Eden's gate, preventing any possibility of Adam and Eve returning, at least on their terms. They had 'died', and the entire human race fell with them (1 Corinthians 15:22). Only a new birth can bring spiritual life into such an appalling situation (John 3:6,7).

With the passage of time, man discovered that such was his estrangement from God he no longer desired fellowship with his Creator. Even worse, he believed he did not need God either in life or in death. The thief was in that category, 'dead' to the dying Christ even as he was 'dead' to the living God.

The tragedy of the unregenerate thief has been repeated in the lives of a myriad of sinners throughout the centuries: so hardened in sin, the unbelief so brazen, the conscience is seared and the moral nerve ends have withered and died. At that point, God quietly switches off the light, locks the door and walks away. It is the ultimate, and eternal, rejection: the sinner of his Creator, and the Creator of his creature. As Jesus once chillingly said to the persistently unbelieving: 'ye . . . shall die in your sins. . .' (John 8:21). There can be nothing worse than that.

If the criminal experienced this ultimate ignominy (and the final verdict is not man's to ascertain), it was not until he had been provided with every opportunity to realize Who and what he was rejecting. Providence had placed him in a unique position, a close observer of the atoning sacrifice for sin. While the Saviour was in the throes of paying the full penalty of man's curse under the broken law, the lawbreaker was within earshot; but no cry for help was forthcoming.

During his ministry Jesus had compassionately bidden the sinner, 'heavy laden' under the pressure of a stricken conscience, to come to him. Whilst on the cross, the invitation was still open.

Therefore, if the thief suffered the ultimate divine rejection, as appears likely, it was an irony of immense proportions.

He died an acutely lonely man, engulfed in shadows where no hope penetrated, unable and equally unwilling to seek any help for his soul. He could not have ignored the sounds of the ground rumbling and the rocks rolling down the hillsides, but it appears he remained adamant in his rejection of the Saviour to the bitter end.

Within minutes his wasted life, for which a further account would have been made to his Maker, was over. His friend 'slept', but he died. Far from his sufferings ending, they had barely begun. Everlasting torment stretched out before him. The thief's only hope had been so near, yet so far away. With Judas Iscariot, he must remain history's greatest human tragedy.

7.

THE FAITHFUL FRIENDS

'A friend loveth at all times'
(Proverbs 17: 17).

(i) THE GRIEVING GALILEANS

*'Now there stood by the cross of Jesus his mother, and his
mother's sister, Mary the wife of Cleophas, and Mary
Magdalene. When Jesus therefore saw his mother,
and the disciple standing by, whom he loved, he saith
unto his mother, Woman, behold thy son! Then saith
he to the disciple, Behold thy mother! And from that
hour that disciple took her unto his own home'*
(John 19:25–27).

What sympathy Jesus received from those gathered on Golgotha's
hill came from a little knot of people who stood silently and
patiently at the foot of his cross. The group consisted mainly of
women, 'his mother, and his mother's sister, Mary the wife of
Cleophas, and Mary Magdalene'; but there was a man with them
to provide a modicum of comfort in what was a very harrowing
situation. He was the apostle John, Mary of Nazareth's nephew,
the son of her sister Salome.

Between the five there existed a bond which drew them to such
a spot, a fervent love for Jesus, and therefore an interest in what
was happening to him. Second-hand reports would not have suf-
ficed. They persisted in standing beside him throughout his suffering, an act of courage which was the token of their affection and
one undoubtedly appreciated by Jesus himself. His mother posi-
tioned herself beside her son as any mother would, and received

consolation from her friends who were particularly affectionate towards her. These included Mary of Magdala, whose deliverance from devils assured Jesus of a central place in her devotion (Luke 8:2).

The little group of Galileans were unsophisticated country folk. The sight of three men being brutally killed within a few feet appalled and horrified them, but the fact that Jesus was one of the victims proved almost too much to bear.

This was especially so for his mother Mary, who remembered the moment over thirty years before when Simeon warned her about this day. Then, as a six-week-old infant, Jesus was cradled in the arms of the godly old man. Within the Temple precincts he had solemnly prophesied: 'Behold, this child is set for the fall and rising again of many in Israel; and for a sign which shall be spoken against. (Yea, a sword shall pierce through thy own soul also,) . . .' (Luke 2:34,35). Golgotha's 'sword' penetrated very deeply.

John remembered Jesus' words the previous night, as he had broken the Passover bread in pieces: 'Take, eat: this is my body.' They were spoken with great solemnity and had a profound effect upon the eleven men present. They were beginning to understand as far as they were able, and probably for the first time, what Jesus had meant earlier in the evening when speaking of his imminent departure.

At Golgotha, observing the agonized expression on his Master's face and listening to the groans generated by unremitted suffering, John now understood. Jesus also lay passively on the palm of a hand like the piece of bread. It was the giant hand of the Father, who orders all events in accordance with his will and purpose. On the cross that hand closed into a fist and tightened its grip. God the Son was in the process of being broken on behalf of others. It was a substitutionary atonement. Unlike Isaac, he was not rescued at the last minute from the 'knife' which hovered over him (Genesis 22:1-14)!

His mother and her friends watched the process from close quarters. There was nothing they could do to help or comfort him in his distress, and certainly no way in which they could assist him in his atoning work. They could only watch helplessly, and pray earnestly.

It comforted John to realize the significance of that moment in the upper room when Jesus had distributed the pieces of bread to his friends in turn. As he did so he had said, 'I have desired to eat this passover with you before I suffer' (Luke 22:15). What an honour to be the recipient of such a gracious invitation!

It was clear that his affection for them was shared equally. They, like every disciple since, were only too aware of their lowly position. They were ordinary sinners, yet the Son of God desired to share the symbol of his saving benefits with them. There was no mistaking what he had said to them earlier in the evening: 'Greater love hath no man than this, that a man lay down his life for his friends' (John 15:13). His was a love unrivalled, as he lay broken under heaven's righteous indignation as the Substitute for his people. It was the fulfilment of God's words to his covenant people: 'I have loved thee with an everlasting love: therefore with lovingkindness have I drawn thee' (Jeremiah 31:3).

At Golgotha, there was much violence and a great deal of blood. The cross was liberally spattered with it, as were the hands of the soldiers who had nailed their victim to it. Blood dripped from his hands and feet, and ran down his back from the wounds inflicted by the scourging. The ground upon which the cross stood was soon blood red, until the rains erased the evidence.

John reflected further upon the events of a few hours earlier, when in Gethsemane's garden he had heard Jesus speaking to the Father about his 'cup' of suffering (Matthew 26:39). John, together with his brother James and their friend Peter, had been separated by Jesus from the other apostles and permitted to enter the garden with him. There, he instructed the three to pray while he made his way deeper into the copse of olive trees, a stone's throw away (Luke 22:40,41).

They had watched him walk slowly from them, until suddenly he sunk to his knees in prayer. They could hear his voice: 'O my Father, if it be possible, let this cup pass from me: nevertheless not as I will, but as thou wilt' (Matthew 26:39). It was a cry of sombre intensity.

Christ's agony had begun at that point. He had told John and the other two the reasons for it: 'My soul is exceeding sorrowful, even unto death' (Matthew 26:38). Perfect obedience to the extremity of the Father's will wrestled with the frailties of the flesh. But no one has ever been confronted with such a conflict, which explained why his closest friends were unable to encourage him. His situation was not helped by the knowledge that even at that moment Judas was on his way with a large company in an act of betrayal.

Jesus was a solitary figure. No one has experienced such intense loneliness. The supreme sacrifice was called for, with heaven observing the scene and Satan seeking to overthrow the Father's plan. Jesus was at the centre of the struggle. He alone had the keys of heaven's gates. Without his lonely battle, it would remain for ever beyond the reach of man, and there could be no second chance. Conversely, his victory would secure eternal redemption for a myriad from each generation, and from the four corners of the earth. The hymnist has penned the situation graphically, in a hymn which John and his friends could quite easily have written:

> *It was alone the Saviour prayed*
> *In dark Gethsemane;*
> *Alone he drained the bitter cup*
> *And suffered there for me.*
> *Alone, alone, he bore it all alone;*
> *He gave himself to save his own,*
> *He suffered, bled and died alone, alone.*

John's feelings were probably mixed. He remembered all too clearly with what gravity Jesus had predicted that his disciples would forsake him when their fellowship was important to him, and run away seeking safety for themselves (Matthew 26:56). John felt ashamed, if not hypocritical, that he had the effrontery to turn up at the last minute. He who a few hours earlier had affectionately leaned his head against Jesus' chest, now felt embarrassed to look at him.

What he saw moved him profoundly. Jesus' appearance told the story of his humiliation. The strain of the long night hours, the prolonged interrogations, the brutal hands, the scourging, the accumulative exhaustion, the hatred, the soul's sorrow: all this guaranteed that there would be 'no beauty that we should desire him'. The sight sickened John, and even more so the women with him. They stared at their Master in shocked silence.

Seven centuries earlier, the prophet had declared: 'his visage was so marred more than any man, and his form more than the sons of men' (Isaiah 52:14). The crown still clung to his head, kept in position by the penetration into the flesh of the sharp thorns. His dying eyes were sunken behind a bruised face stained with blood. His mouth remained open as he gasped for breath. His lips and tongue were dry and swollen, and when he intimated that he was thirsty, his request was whispered almost imperceptibly. Clearly, his strength had 'dried up'.

But John's obvious grief, shared by his companions, would not last long. Within weeks, he heard the mighty wind of the Spirit and was present as thousands in a day received salvation. He and his fellow apostles were remarkably empowered. They preached to the vast crowds who had assembled in Jerusalem for the feast of Pentecost, declaring that the phenomenon they were witnessing was due to the fact of Christ's resurrection and ascension to glory.

Quietness settled over skull hill once more. The raging storm departed as quickly as it had arrived, and the darkened sky was swept away by the shafts of light from the sun. Birds sang again. It was all over! Golgotha squelched with mud, the crosses dripped with water, and the bedraggled few glanced around to see who had survived the trauma of the previous three hours.

The centurion and his four men, who during the earthquake had been at full stretch keeping the crosses in position, must have been surprised to discover they were not alone. Jesus' mother and her companions had kept a lonely and silent vigil beside him through-out his ordeal, a courage and devotion which must have impressed the soldiers.

The centurion was now united to them by a new-found faith,

and together they watched Jesus who was clearly only a breath or two away from the paradise he had mentioned earlier to one of the thieves. It therefore came as a surprise to hear a thin whisper, one which was directed towards his mother, in an unforgettable moment of tender simplicity.

Jesus had suffered the ravages of human brutality, and had surrendered himself to the crucible of eternal retribution, but his dying thoughts were for the future welfare of his mother. His head had slumped forward, his eyes were almost closed, but they turned from Mary to John – 'behold thy son!'; and then from John to Mary – 'Behold thy mother!' (John 19:26,27).

Shortly afterwards, Mary left the dismal area with her friends to await developments, and to begin a new life in the bosom of John's family.

The grieved, trembling and sickened women having left the scene, John saw one of the soldiers callously strike Jesus' dead body with a spear (John 19:34). The Roman did not know it, but his action not only illustrated his hatred for the Jews, but gave grounds for two other important matters. To the world it would prove that Jesus had actually died while on the cross (although of course not as a result of the spear thrust), and it would remind the church of the relevance of biblical prophecy, '. . . and they shall look upon me whom they have pierced . . .' (Zechariah 12:10). John also noticed that from the wound in Jesus' side poured blood and water, providing every Christian from that moment with a reason for repentance and thanksgiving:

> *Let the water and the blood,*
> *From thy riven side which flowed,*
> *Be of sin the double cure,*
> *Cleanse me from its guilt and power.*

Following the traumatic events of an extraordinary day, a stillness settled over Golgotha. It was the quietness of the cemetery, a silence broken only by the muffled sounds of the centurion and his men putting the finishing touches to their arduous duties. This would include breaking the legs of the thieves that death might be hastened. It was the final cruelty of the day, insisted upon by the Sanhedrin, whose members having killed God's Son were nevertheless careful to keep his Sabbath!

(ii) THE CARING COUNCILLORS

'And after this Joseph of Arimathaea, being a disciple of Jesus,
but secretly for fear of the Jews, besought Pilate that he might
take away the body of Jesus: and Pilate gave him leave.
He came therefore, and took the body of Jesus.
And there came also Nicodemus . . .'
(John 19:38, 39).

It was late afternoon, Israel's twilight, and a group of men could be seen nearby. They moved very slowly from the hill, their progress hampered by the heaviness of what they carried. It was the body of Jesus, who had been the first of the three victims to die. Even in this simple fact, one which surprised Pilate, Scripture was fulfilled, for the soldiers had not needed to break Jesus' legs (Psalm 34:20). He was the unblemished sacrificial Lamb, who remained 'without spot' throughout his atoning ministry on the cross.

Nobody knows how many were in the party which made its way from skull hill. John was probably one of them. Having been present at about the time Jesus' body was taken from the cross, he would certainly have wanted to assist. There were also two important members of the Sanhedrin, Joseph of Arimathea and Nicodemus. As well as these were other men, probably servants, to help in the main task of carrying the body.

Joseph and Nicodemus had been secret disciples of Jesus, until they were prompted by his death to own publicly their allegiance to him. That his followers existed within the ruling body of Judaism was made known to Jesus at the beginning of his ministry. Nicodemus, under cover of darkness, met and encouraged him by reporting the fact: 'WE know that thou art a teacher come from God' (John 3:2). The teaching concerning new birth was first discussed at that clandestine meeting.

The reason why the two high-ranking councillors remained in the shadows is not difficult to discover. As we have seen, the Sanhedrin consisted of Jesus' most fervent opponents whose members had spent much time in plotting his death. They considered him an apostate, and a danger to traditional beliefs. It was not the time to be seen supporting him. In any case, the Sadducees like the high priests Caiaphas and his father-in-law Annas did not believe in a messianic hope or even in an after-life. They were therefore unlikely to treat kindly anyone who did.

The ordinary people were also afraid to support Jesus, fearing the possibility of excommunication from the synagogue. It took courage to be closely identified with him anywhere in Israel, let alone in the heart of the council. At one point, Nicodemus made his presence felt in the parliament by seeking simple justice for his Master, but his words were rejected with a sneer. To have hidden one's light then in the fearful atmosphere generated by the Sanhedrin, although not to be commended, was certainly understandable.

It was probably the appalling behaviour of the priests at Calvary which caused Joseph and Nicodemus, and others, to lift their heads above the parapet (Acts 15:5). As soon as he heard Jesus had died, Joseph courageously stepped out by faith. He saw the need to secure custody of his Lord's body, despite what his colleagues in the Sanhedrin would say. In defying them, Joseph risked his career and reputation among the Jews.

He appealed directly to Pilate, but Joseph took more than one risk in doing so. By making a request to the Roman authorities he placed himself under an obligation to them, or even the possibility of death. Joseph also realized that Pilate might demand a bribe, putting him in an impossible position. Despite all this, however, the strengthening of his faith supplied him with the courage to go ahead with his plan. His commitment to Christ now meant more to him than the anger of the Jews or the Romans, his reputation, his career or even his life.

He knew the matter was urgent. The Sabbath was only hours away, and God's law demanded that the body of an executed man was not to remain throughout the night on the gibbet. In any case, this would not be an ordinary Sabbath, but a 'high day' part of the Passover week. Strictness in observing the law's demands was paramount to all Jews, and not least to a distinguished member of Judaism's religious parliament. Jesus' body had to be entombed as quickly as possible.

Pilate's granting of the request, once he was satisfied his prisoner was dead, was unusual. It brought great joy to Joseph and the entire community of disciples, but it implied a sympathy for Jesus from the Roman governor which they would not have expected. Perhaps the meeting between the two had impressed Pilate more than he would have liked to admit. Certainly, his insistence about the wording of the official accusation might give credence to this view (John 18:28-38; 19:21,22).

The group did not have far to go with their precious load, no doubt having informed Mary and her companions what they intended doing. Within sight of skull hill was a garden belonging to Joseph. Being a wealthy man, it is possible to believe that it would have been typical of its kind: a peaceful haven luxuriant with flowers, olive trees and blossom. The two locations contrasted sharply, the grotesque discordance of Golgotha giving way to nature's beauty and tranquillity.

Joseph guided his companions to a quiet and shaded corner. There, freshly hewn into the solid rock was a tomb, and nearby a large boulder which was to serve as the door to the opening. Joseph had ordered this tomb for himself, where in death he would be as close to the holy city as possible. But now he had found a more urgent and important need for it. The tomb, being new, was not associated with death's decay; Jesus' burial was as 'virgin' as his birth had been.

It was small, just large enough for what was required. Not everyone in the group was able to enter, but those who did laid his body reverently on the rocky niche cut away for that purpose. They then went outside to allow Joseph and Nicodemus entry into the confined space. The sun was slowly setting, time was at a premium, and there was still a ritual to perform.

Probably because of their former timidity in publicly supporting their Master, the two well-to-do, cultured and distinguished rulers insisted on carrying out the necessary duties themselves (John 19:40). They must have been conscious of the fact that poor and uneducated disciples had proved braver and more loyal to the Saviour. Joseph and Nicodemus failed their Lord in his life: now within the tomb they felt a need to express their devotion to him in his death.

With great care they first washed his bruised body, 'bruised for our iniquities', discoloured by dried blood and sweat. Then they covered it with the spices, 'an hundred pound weight', which Nicodemus had bought for the occasion. The spices were expensive, but he had learned the mistake of mounting up earthly treasures which risked being lost through corruption or theft.

Instead, Nicodemus had come to realize that the true wealth lies not in coinage but in Christ. In the light of that, how 'poor' the chief ruler had been! In fact, during their first meeting Jesus had expressed astonishment at his ignorance of spiritual matters (John 3:10). However, Nicodemus soon appreciated the gracious appeal of the gospel. The Redeemer was far 'wealthier' than the ruler, but had 'become poor' that Nicodemus in his abject poverty of soul might inherit the riches of heaven (2 Corinthians 8:9).

There was only one thing left for him to do. Like Mary of Bethany with her 'very costly' ointment with which she had lovingly anointed her Saviour, Nicodemus also desired to express his devotion and gratitude. The expensive spices were liberally sprinkled upon the Saviour's body.

The task having been completed, with the clean white linen cloth wound around the body and the napkin wrapped about the head of Jesus, Joseph and Nicodemus paused to meditate.

Within the precincts of the tomb, the two councillors stared at the body lying before them. Three years had passed since the name of Jesus of Nazareth had first come to their attention, years which proved to be unique in the annals of even Israel's remarkable history. She had harboured in her midst the Son of God, the precise expression of the Father's mind and the radiance of his glory, yet the Servant whose substitutionary atonement would 'justify many'. The plan, purposes and promises of God, and the hopes and dreams of his people: centuries of expectancy were fulfilled in Jesus.

The two brethren left the tomb. Few words would have been spoken, but their thoughts were plentiful. The immediate uncertainty cast a gloom over the community of nervous disciples, but heaven's anthem had already been composed: 'Worthy is the Lamb that was slain to receive power, and riches, and wisdom, and strength, and honour, and glory, and blessing.'

Soon, these shouts of acclamation would be joined by a myriad more, 'a great multitude, which no man could number, of all nations, and kindreds, and people, and tongues . . . saying, Salvation to our God which sitteth upon the throne, and unto the Lamb' (Revelation 5:12; 7:9,10).

Counting the specks of dust upon the earth would be as simple as numbering heaven's blood-bought citizens! They gather at the throne adoring the Lamb, whose glory they share. Earth has never seen such exquisite beauty, nor heard such glorious sounds, as those which have been awaiting the redeemed since 'the beginning of the world'.

With the others who had waited outside, the two friends pushed the large boulder along its gully until it covered the aperture. The body of Jesus was entombed, having 'made his grave with the wicked, and with the rich in his death'. With the sun disappearing behind the hills, the group left the garden to await events.

They would not have to wait for long. Had not their Lord told them the length of time (Matthew 16:21)? Through the uneasiness of that weekend the triumphant voice of Isaiah could have been heard across the centuries, had it not been drowned in the disciples' despondency: 'He will swallow up death in victory; and the Lord God will wipe away tears from off all faces; and the rebuke of his people shall he take away from off all the earth: for the Lord hath spoken it' (Isaiah 25:8).

APPENDIX

It was at the close of his very long life that John's view of his Master was elevated still further. He was exiled on an island in the Aegean Sea called Patmos, a Roman penal colony, because of his influence over the Christian communities. There he received a visit from his risen and ascended Lord, before whom he collapsed in awe and wonder. Tenderly, and compassionately, Jesus assisted John to his feet (Revelation 1:10-18).

How different the Lord appeared from when John had seen him at Golgotha! No longer was he naked, the Slave dying for the enslaved, but was dressed in a garment similar to the one John had often seen him wearing. There was a fundamental difference though. Jesus' belt of cord or leather had been replaced by one of gold. He who 'took on him the seed of Abraham' was 'made like unto his brethren'; and he who 'was in all points tempted like as we are, yet without sin', had ascended into heaven and brought 'many sons unto glory' through his atoning sacrifice (Hebrews 2 & 4). In other words, standing before John was the eternal King-Priest (Zechariah 6:12,13).

At the foot of the cross, John saw Jesus covered in blood and bruises. On Patmos, he gazed in amazement at his Lord. He was obliged to shelter his eyes with an arm like a man staring at the sun. Christ's crown of thorns was absent, his head not bloodied and bowed, but a resplendent snowy white. Eternal Wisdom! of whom it is said, 'I was set up from everlasting, from the beginning, or ever the earth was. When there were no depths, I was brought forth; when there were no fountains abounding with water. Before the mountains were settled, before the hills was I brought forth' (Proverbs 8:23-25).

If the Jews 'require a sign', the 'Greeks' have always sought wisdom (1 Corinthians 1:17-31). This present age is famous for its delight in discovery and its confidence in acquired wisdom. Science and philosophy juggle with armfuls of theories, but they merely lean upon wisdom gleaned from others. This, however, presupposes that there is a Source from which that wisdom has come.

A mere glance around the universe should be enough to impress and amaze the fair-minded individual. What Mind is there capable of producing such order and beauty? Creation's colourful display, from the vastness of seemingly endless space, and the sparkling galaxies of mysterious stars, to the petal on the smallest flower: all this, and much more, is the backcloth upon which Eternal Wisdom has painted his designs.

Like John, the apostle Paul also sees Jesus in the full flush of his majesty as the One 'in whom are hid all the treasures of wisdom and knowledge' (Colossians 2:3). When learned men stand one day before him at the bar of judgment, they will realize (perhaps too late) that he has always been the inspirer of their studies: 'When he prepared the heavens, I was there: when he set a compass upon the face of the depth: when he established the clouds above: when he strengthened the foundations of the deep . . . Then I was by him, as one brought up with him: and I was daily his delight, rejoicing always before him' (Proverbs 8:27,28,30). Where indeed is the wise, the scribe or the disputer of this world? God has declared it all 'foolish' (1 Corinthians 1:20).

Christ's eyes, mirroring his sufferings whilst on the cross, reflected the flaming fires of divine holiness on Patmos (Revelation 1:14). The sight of them was dazzling to John, like sun shining on freshly fallen snow. No one can look into the eyes of the God-man. His presence disturbs and embarrasses the sinner. He, for whom the hosts in heaven were created, and to whom all praise and adoration is eternally directed (Revelation 4:11), has no equal among men or angels (Revelation 5:12-14).

Even before Christ spoke, John realized he had cause to examine himself. God examines us all: every nook and cranny. In the humility of the Son of man, we taste our arrogance (John 13:4-6). In the Son's perfect obedience to the Father's will, we are made aware of our innate stubbornness and pride (John 5:30). Christ's fulness of love exposes our lack of it. His stainless character serves to underline the truth of man's natural depravity.

Christ is the yardstick by which mankind is measured in the sight and light of heaven. His influence cannot be avoided intellectually, nor morally or ethically. All this, before he opens his mouth to reveal his verdict!

John had it revealed to him that the ascended Lord is not only the yardstick. A yardstick is impersonal. The Lord of Glory also uses his eyes, and they bored into his soul. John was being searched for the slightest imperfection. The angry flames of divine holiness instantly consume that which lies outside of the framework of perfection. God is a 'consuming fire' (Hebrews 12:29). There is an immediate reaction against sin. As fire creates terror in those engulfed in it, so the sinner not justified in God's sight by faith alone faces the full fury of holy wrath. It is indeed 'a fearful thing to fall into the hands of the living God' (Hebrews 10:31).

Unable to glance for long at his Lord's eyes aflame with holiness, John bowed his head and, in doing so, noticed the feet once pierced with nails (Psalm 22:16). Now, although still bearing their prints (Luke 24:39,40), Christ's feet possess the radiance of molten bronze (Revelation 1:15). The God-man has the power and authority to stamp firmly upon all his enemies.

The destiny of mankind is entirely in his hands, and he will crush all rivals (Revelation 19:11-16). The torments of the eternally damned are under his direct control (Revelation 1:17,18), as the everlasting bliss of the redeemed is the fruit of his atoning work. Jesus has left his footsteps deep in humanity's soil. Pity those who do not know him! Created to worship him and having not done so, they enter the presence of the King of kings and Lord of lords. He tramples them into eternal fires (Revelation 14:14-20).

That voice! A mere whisper in its weakness at Golgotha, on Patmos isle it had 'the sound of many waters' (Revelation 1:15). Like the millions of gallons which form a giant waterfall, the sounds are ever present. From birth to death and beyond the grave, the authoritative voice of Christ follows us. We cannot hide from it, try as we might. It whispers to our conscience. It also cries aloud from the landscape, bidding us to observe 'his eternal power and Godhead' (Romans 1:18-20).

This was the Presence which caused such turmoil when Jesus walked in the midst of men (Matthew 7:28,29). The people were amazed, critical, hateful and divided; but they were never indifferent (John 7:43). He called sinners to himself in a way which, in any other, would have sounded egotistical.

Deliberately applying the name of God to illustrate his 'power over all flesh' (John 17:2), Jesus informs the world that he is the glorious 'I AM' (Exodus 3:14): 'I AM the living bread' (John 6:51), 'before Abraham was' (John 8:58), 'the door of salvation' (John 10:9), 'the good shepherd' (John 10:14), 'the resurrection' (John 11:25), 'the light' (John 12:46), 'the way, the truth, and the life' (John 14:6), 'the true vine' (John 15:1), 'the King' (John 18:37)—in fact, GOD! On Patmos, the sum total of his claims was expressed in his statement to John: 'I am Alpha and Omega, the beginning and the ending . . . which is, and which was, and which is to come, the Almighty' (Revelation 1:8).

John looked beyond the island and envisaged the return of God's triumphant Son to the world which rejected and crucified him. At Golgotha, his mouth was swollen and his voice reduced to a whisper, but John was permitted to see that issuing from it was 'a sharp twoedged sword' (Revelation 1:16). When he unveils his awesomeness, it will be as One 'taking vengeance on them that know not God, and that obey not [his] gospel' (2 Thessalonians 1:8). The 'sword' wielded so efficiently by the Judge has a sharp cutting edge.

However, the second advent will not only be an occasion for weeping, wailing and gnashing of teeth (Matthew 25:30-33). The apostle Paul encouraged his friend Titus to look 'for that blessed hope, and the glorious appearing of the great God and our Saviour Jesus Christ' (Titus 2:13).

A child of God has every right to look forward to that 'glorious' occasion, when the book of life will be opened and his name read out as one redeemed by the precious blood of his Saviour. Paul possessed a humble confidence, which redemption assures: 'Henceforth there is laid up for me a crown of righteousness, which the Lord, the righteous judge, shall give me at that day: and not to me only, but unto all them also that love his appearing' (2 Timothy 4:8).

Other titles published by the
Evangelical Press of Wales

Also by Peter Trumper

'They Beheld His Glory'

Although the story of the birth of the Lord Jesus
Christ is always a cause of wonder and worship to
the Christian, this book will further enhance our
praise and adoration as the author leads us to view
that birth through the eyes of those who were there
to behold his glory.

The author's vivid style of writing and extensive
knowledge of the Scriptures makes it both an
instructive and devotional book that enlightens the
mind and warms the heart.

What is Truth?
An Outline of the Christian Faith

Bryan A. Williams

In this book of just 68 pages Dr Bryan Williams has managed to give us a straightforward and wide-ranging explanation of all the major fundamentals of the Christian Faith.

What is truth? is one of the most readable primers in Christian Theology available. It will prove beneficial to new Christians as well as to believers of many years standing seeking a better grounding in the Faith.